# Through Adversity
# to Attainment

Autobiography of
## William A. Franklin
Compiled from 1967 to 2003

Note for Librarians: A cataloguing record for this book is available from Library and Archives Canada at www.collectionscanada.ca/amicus/index-e.html
ISBN 1-4120-6004-4

*Printed in Victoria, BC, Canada. Printed on paper with minimum 30% recycled fibre. Trafford's print shop runs on "green energy" from solar, wind and other environmentally-friendly power sources.*

# TRAFFORD

*Offices in Canada, USA, Ireland and UK*
This book was published *on-demand* in cooperation with Trafford Publishing. On-demand publishing is a unique process and service of making a book available for retail sale to the public taking advantage of on-demand manufacturing and Internet marketing. On-demand publishing includes promotions, retail sales, manufacturing, order fulfilment, accounting and collecting royalties on behalf of the author.

**Book sales for North America and international:**
Trafford Publishing, 6E–2333 Government St.,
Victoria, BC v8t 4p4 CANADA
phone 250 383 6864 (toll-free 1 888 232 4444)
fax 250 383 6804; email to orders@trafford.com
**Book sales in Europe:**
Trafford Publishing (uk) Ltd., Enterprise House, Wistaston Road Business Centre,
Wistaston Road, Crewe, Cheshire cw2 7rp UNITED KINGDOM
phone 01270 251 396 (local rate 0845 230 9601)
facsimile 01270 254 983; orders.uk@trafford.com
**Order online at:**
trafford.com/05-0905

10 9 8 7 6 5 4 3 2

# Table of Contents

# Acknowledgements

Without the vigorous persuasion of my niece, Margaret, and her husband Peter Green, their daughter, Helen, and son, Jonathon, this memoir would never have been completed.

During my years with the Pacific Lumber Inspection Bureau, I travelled extensively, and many evenings were spent in hotel and motel rooms without follow-up paperwork from the day's activities. On such occasions, I would take a sheet of the inn's writing paper, and scribbled out episodes of my experiences.

From these papers, several family members, diligently worked to decipher and type out my scrawl into legible articles to file. I wish to express my sincere gratitude to my sister-in-law, Ollie Franklin and her sister, Jean Mair (deceased), and to my niece Maggie Sim (also deceased), for their help. Thanks also to the Langley Writers Guild, for guidance and encouragement when I was a member, and to my daughter, Rosalind Plumtree, for final editing.

Thanks also to Peggy Matthews for the tremendous job of transferring the text onto computer, breaking it down into chapters, as well as doing the layout, and saving to disks. A special thank you to Dennis Johnson, President of the Alder Grove Heritage Society, for his expertise and time spent with the illustrations and to the staff of the Society, Tim Johnson and Diane MacKenzie. Tim assisted with the photographs and Diane devoted a great deal of time to making sure all errors were corrected and to providing additional material such as the Table of Contents.

Above all else, I am indebted to my partner, Phyllis, for her care, devotion, and encouragement given to me, through many adversities.

Medals Received:
1939-1945 Star – for over 180 days combat service
Pacific Star for service in the Pacific Campaign
1939-1945 Medal – for full service 1939-1945
International Prisoner of War Medal

# Preface

I dedicate this book to my family and friends who have made requests that I should relate my beliefs and experiences of a lucky and fruitful life.

You are about to read of my life as I remember the early days. I realized my parents were to control me in those things pertaining to what I could or could not do, with restraint. These are events and happenings that involved me, and I have only referred to a person by name who was actually part of a joint experience.

In the Air Force, I was subservient to the end, trusting my services would be sufficient to help bring about victory. Our facilities, located some ten to fifteen miles behind the front lines, were used to service and maintain the aircraft. At no time did I hear about or know of other units working with us, and throughout the campaign, we were kept in ignorance of the facts. We were left to draw our own conclusions as our strength became depleted.

Throughout the prisoner-of-war years, each of us was treated individually, until punishment was handed out—then everyone suffered. From those years onward, I have tried to fulfill all my responsibilities to each endeavour, and to my family.

My beliefs and statements are solely my own conclusions, and in no way intended to implicate any other individual. It seems ironic that everything I encountered resolved to no avail.


William A. Franklin
October 1997

# 1
—

## *My Parents, Childhood Days & the General Strike*

**M**y mother was born in Chelsea, London, England (the eldest of eleven children of William and Emma Bridge) and enjoyed a good childhood. She spoke frequently of her schooling and her willingness to learn. The teachers were strict, but they found pleasant ways to keep the students interested. She remembered being elated over the way she could lead the girls over the gym horse with the use of a springboard. This created a standard the other girls found hard to meet. She was fortunate to have had private piano and organ lessons, and later played for Sunday school classes and some church services at Holy Trinity, Sloane Square, London. Eventually, she passed through Chelsea Polytechnic School with flying colours.

Mother was an attractive lady, five feet, ten inches tall. Her given name of Florence soon became Florrie when she accepted a position as Secretary and Lady's Companion to a Miss Harvey. They traveled the British Isles, but never overseas. Mother always had a soft spot in her heart for Inverness, Scotland. She never let me forget that "the finest English is spoken in Inverness."

On one such trip to Llandrindod, North Wales, the butler of the private residence where they were staying teased my mother into riding a bicycle. This she had never done before, and after the butler had enticed her to sit on it, he gave her instructions on how to balance, steer, and brake. Then, with a little push, he started her on her way down the hill. The bicycle gained momentum, Mother started to shriek, and the butler started shouting, "Brake! Brake!" but to no avail. At the foot of the hill was the village duck pond, and Mother, holding on with all her might, steered straight into the water. She was thrown over the handlebars and came up, sitting in the middle of the pond! From that day on, strict orders forbade any further association with employees at any residence.

World War I broke out, and when the German Zeppelins (airships) started to bomb London, one of the first bombs that fell obliterated the front of the house next door to Miss Harvey's residence. She promptly shuttered up her London home and went to Oxford, taking over a part of a house on the Banbury Road, adjacent to Norham Road and Norham Gardens. Mother stayed with her.

Because Oxford is just sixty-two and a half miles from Paddington, London, it was possible to make the journey in one hour. Fifteen minutes more on the underground train put Mother in Sloane Square and within walking distance of her parent's home. Naturally, conversation gradually increased on each visit with regard to the nice young postman working Florrie's route. Her brothers and sisters soon became aware of a secret within the household, and just as soon as the word got out, she was teased into producing him for their inspection.

So Dad made his first trip to London and met the family that accepted him warmly.

My father, Edwin Franklin, was born on December 29, 1892, in an old English village called Tackley, located eight miles north of Oxford. Tackley is nestled in a valley by the river Cherwell. The buildings of stone with thatched roofs are still in use today. An old Norman Church, St. Nicholas, complete with peal of bells, sits on the side of a hill, above the village, overlooking the rich farmland.

These country folk had their own distinct dialect; so close to the university at Oxford, but far removed in their English language. When something was good, my dad would say it is "top-ole!" In greeting, he would say, "How be doing then old cock?" or "How are you, ducks?"

As a boy, he sang with a very good soprano voice in the church choir, performing such works as the "Messiah" and "Elijah." Later, he learned the art of bell ringing. He did not advance beyond the old schoolhouse, but became a professional gardener.

My father could be quite a stubborn man, and this stubbornness almost cost him his life. His refusal to seek help for abdominal pain resulted in a ruptured appendix and peritonitis, demanding an eight-mile ambulance dash to the Radcliffe Infirmary at Oxford. The doctor, anticipating further surgery, used clamps instead of stitches, which Dad ripped open in his sleep. The second visit to surgery and closing up the incision, caused a weakening of the stomach wall, which affected him the rest of his life.

World War I started. Dad was immediately conscripted into the 4th Battalion—Oxford and Bucks Light Infantry. They were stationed at the Portsmouth Barracks where they began their orientation and training in combat skills. During a bayonet practice, Dad was stabbing at a straw-stuffed dummy when his old operation scar popped open. He collapsed.

Unable to comply with the Sergeant's command, "Stand on your feet!" they finally carried him to the base hospital. The doctor stitched up the old wound and gave him a period of time for recuperation. He was then assigned to kitchen duties for his platoon, being considered unfit for combat.

The kitchen was situated in the basement. This meant eight flights of stairs had to be climbed to reach his platoon's dining area in their quarters on the fourth floor. All food had to be carried up from the kitchen since there were no dumbwaiters or elevators in the building.

Dad fulfilled his kitchen duties for approximately three months. When carrying a large iron pot of potatoes, he collapsed again, on the third flight of stairs. The wound had reopened. These duties were considered "light duties," but with Dad's inability to handle them he was brought before a medical board. The board's decision gave him a discharge, "being unfit for military service."

With his army commitment behind him, Dad returned home to his parents and the village doctor. The doctor, with the help of his professional contacts, designed a body belt for Dad. It was along the lines of a corset, complete with a number of steel stays built in to support the whole abdomen. It was surprisingly comfortable and gave him all the support that was necessary throughout the rest of his life.

Dad was directed to the employment office for work within the Civil Service. They placed him with the Oxford Post Office in a temporary position as a postman. Six days a week he bicycled the eight miles to work and home again in the evening. Mail sorters placed the letters and small packages into the appropriate pigeonholes for each street. The postmen in turn, took those within their designated area, collated them by number, and set out on delivery. The public busses carried them to their respective districts where they continued on foot.

Postal deliveries were made three or four times a day, the first one in time for breakfast and the last around five in the afternoon. If material of an urgent nature was received first thing in the morning, a reply could be written, posted for the noon collection, and delivered that same day. Better still, a reply could be made by telegram. Written and then handed across the post office counter, it would be phoned through to its destination within a few minutes. The only time factor would be at the receiving end, where the message was typed and dispatched via a boy on a bicycle.

It was within Dad's delivery area that Miss Harvey had taken up residence. Due to one small package that would not pass through the letter slot in the front door, he had to ring the doorbell to make the delivery. Dad pulled on the polished brass knob housed in the doorjamb. It was connected by a wire passing through a series of pulley wheels hung close to the ceiling, to a bell that swung on a large spring in the service room. Above the bell was fitted a box of individual signals in the form of stars, known as the "Bell Telegraph." When a knob was pulled, one of the stars would swing denoting which room or doorbell, was calling for service. Florrie was talking with the housemaid in the hallway, and when the door opened, she saw Edwin for the first time.

As the weeks rolled by, they gradually became acquainted. It remains a mystery how they found the opportunity. If Dad failed to meet Florrie on the early morning delivery, there was always a chance of a meeting just a few hours later. The story was often told how they would arrange to go out together. Dad would make the extra ride back to Oxford only to find that Miss Harvey had other ideas. He was out of luck! When they did manage to spend an evening out, they enjoyed going to the theatre.

In spite of their trials and tribulations in the courtship, they finally married on June 12, 1918, at the Holy Trinity Church, Sloane Square, Chelsea, London. They rented a small terrace house in South Oxford, just completed by the builders, (for a cost of thirty pounds), at two shillings and six-pence a week. Dad's wage was adequate, even though his position was still on a temporary basis. Five months later, November 13, 1918, World War I ended. Veterans began to return to the jobs they had held before the war, and there were those never to return.

Mom and Dad had already received the happy news that a baby was on the way, when Dad was called into the office at work. His supervisor advised him of a job transition that was taking place, and requested that he make a decision; one he had not anticipated having to make. He was given time to discuss the question of staying with the post office as a permanent employee, or taking his leave for another type of work. Mom felt her whole world falling apart; their future was at stake.

Although Dad was as healthy as he would ever be, many years of walking and carrying heavy bags of mail were ahead. The alternative was to return to the garden, where the days would be diversified in duties. With the post office, security and steady employment was assured, whereas gardening was questionable.

The decision was centered on his desire to work and be happy doing it, without continual repetition and monotony. With this in mind, he forfeited security and severed his services with the crown. He became the vegetable gardener at St. Edward's School, situated about one and a half miles north of Oxford, on the Woodstock Road. St. Edward's was a boy's grammar school of high renown, with entrance gained mainly through scholarships. During term, three hundred students attended classes, and most of them were members of the Army Cadet Corps.

A stone wall, approximately twelve feet high, surrounded the whole property except for the entrance door of the warden's office, just four or five feet from the boulevard. There was a large gate close to the southern boundary, and a small gate on the north side to service the stores office, situated along the south side of South Parade Road. East of the warden's office, stood the schoolhouse, big hall, and a large classroom block.

Across Woodstock Road, opposite the Warden's quarters, were the beautiful cricket pitch, a striking pavilion, rugby and soccer pitches, and tennis courts. A gravel road, running west parallel to the cricket pitch, continued on to a hand-dug cavity that stored all the harvested, winter root vegetables. They were under timbered roofs and covered with straw to protect them from freezing. Finally, the road reached the large acreage Dad cultivated.

Passing through the farm gates, the road led into the barns. Many grazing acres were along the Oxford-Birmingham Canal. If additional grazing pasture was needed, the herdsman pulled down a drawbridge, counter-balanced above the canal. He then drove the cattle to graze in an area adjacent to Port Meadow. Horses pulling the barges used a small gravel strip running along the banks of the canal. The distance between Oxford and Birmingham is approximately ninety miles, and the canal is still in service, not so much for commerce, but for pleasure boats, most of them powered. Many campers, vacationers, and those seeking weekend relief from the hustle and bustle of city life are a common sight on British waterways today.

The farm was in the capable hands of a man called Oliver, and as on many other similar establishments, his duties were varied and many. Early morning milking from a tuberculosis-tested herd saved the rigors of pasteurization, and the milk was used raw. The kitchen separated it for cream, butter, and cheese. Miss Woodcock, a tall, attractive blonde, would come down to the farm and assist Oliver with the milking and egg collection. She also assisted Dad with some of the seeding and the gathering of crops such as beans, peas, onions, carrots, beets, parsnips and potatoes. The stalls had to be cleaned, two Shire horses (Tom and Job) and a pony (Violet) groomed, and pigs and sties needed attention, as well as sheep, chickens, ducks and geese.

Oliver groomed the playing fields with the Shires pulling the mowers. They had received shrapnel wounds in World War I, when pulling a field gun. Tom was good, settling down with the aftermath, whereas Job suffered from shell shock, and was sensitive to noise. Oliver would spread manure and plow the sections of the gardens, as Dad required. Otherwise, it meant spade digging.

One other man, who had lost his right forearm during the war, worked the greenhouse, roses, and fruit gardens. A large brick wall was covered with espaliers: dessert pears and Victoria plums. There were rows of black and red currants, gooseberries, raspberries and strawberries. He tended the flowerbeds and lawns around the quad. His arm was fitted with a hook which proved invaluable when he was pruning the various bushes and trees.

At the end of the school year, the boys would return to their homes for summer vacation with their parents. This called for Dad to harness up Violet and Tom to the drays to transport the baggage to the railway station. This was repeated in late summer when the new students arrived one week ahead of the returning students, just prior to classes starting in September.

Dad was a keen sportsman and played cricket as a bowler for the College Servant's team. It was amazing to see how active this man was; he could find such energy after toiling all day in the garden!

The moon was approaching its first quarter, and the night air was crisp and clear. For the past few days my mother had been constantly plagued with labour pains and her pregnancy had now reached ten months. She was thirty-two years old, and this was her first child. The home, like most others, had no telephone, so Dad took his bicycle and rode the two miles to the doctor who came in his car. The midwife had arrived, made the necessary preparations, and the birth was well underway before Dad reached home. It was a long and difficult delivery due to unknown complications. I have birthmarks down the right forearm; I'm positive that to put life into me, the doctor held me by the arm and swung me around his head! Suddenly, I was screaming hard and furiously.

Ours was a "terrace" house; one of many in a row attached to each other. To crown it all, the next door neighbour thumped his fist on the wall saying, "Give it some sap!" a phrase that we heard often and never forgot in our household. Mother's only comment about the experience was "We should both be dead!" However, I finally made my entry into this world at one o'clock in the morning on September 29, 1919, (7 lbs. 12 oz.), and was named William Alfred. Mum and Dad made fine progress. I was well displayed to family and friends alike, which included a few "birthday suit" photographs being taken and distributed. It was a fine-looking babe that posed, if I do say so myself!

During my preschool years, I do not recall Mother speaking of any notable family events apart from the births of my two sisters: Mary (June 1, 1921) and Ruth (September 13, 1924). I do remember the morning I started Infant School. Mother fussed over my clothing and hair while I resisted the preparations; I did not want to go.

The New Hinksey Boys and Girls Schools were just a long block away via a walk through the churchyard. Tugged along by the arm, my hand in my Mum's firm grip, I was half running due to her height and stride. We were ushered into a small cloakroom where I hung up my coat before being presented to my first teacher, Miss Alby.

I made good progress at school. There were the usual kid's problems and illnesses, such as measles, which kept me at home, then a very bad attack of mumps. Between the normal learning periods, we would do some exercises and country folk dancing to entertain our parents at afternoon tea. Occasionally, we would march, each of us carrying a little Union Jack on Empire Day, or stand on a busy street corner to wave at King George V and Queen Mary, the Prince of Wales, or some other dignitary. The day came when I finished Infant School, and we boys said goodbye to our female friends. The new term would keep us in segregated classrooms.

# 2

—

## *I Join the Boy's Brigade*

The summer of 1923 was coming to a close when the new boys arrived at St. Edward's School. Among them was Douglas Bader, who had won a scholarship from Temple Grove, a prep school near Eastbourne. He was to become famous as an ace fighter pilot during the war, leading #242 Hurricane Squadron. Through his successes in sports (rugby, soccer, sprinting, and cricket), he quickly advanced into the senior teams.

It was at a cricket match where my father met and played against Bader. At age six (1925), I had watched several games from the pavilion, enjoying the tea time break when I could sit with the players, eating bread and butter, jam or honey, with fancy cakes (half price for me—three pennies). I was known to the staff members as Dad often took me to work, seated on a little saddle attached to the cross bar of his bicycle. Sometimes, I would help him with the harvesting of winter vegetables. Miss Woodcock would take me around the farm and into the kitchens where she gave me a few broken biscuits or other delicacies.

Dad and Oliver ate their lunch in the pavilion's kitchen, situated on the north side. There were windows in three walls which gave a commanding view of the northern grazing pasture, the cattle, and scattered elm trees, and also, the cricket pitch to the east. During one of my visits, we sat eating lunch after working on a hot, sultry morning. Clouds started to roll in, with distant thunder. Within a few minutes, it was raining heavily. We stood up to watch it bouncing inches off the deck, and the cows moving in under cover of the elms. The first blinding flash of lightning, followed immediately with a resounding bang, struck an elm tree, splitting it cleanly in two from the crown to the ground. Simultaneously, two cows were also struck as they stood huddled close to the trunk. They fell to the ground, their carcasses solid blocks of charcoal; a scene I never forgot!

Dad and I had planned to do a tedious task of thinning out the carrots. Removing the small under-developed growth enables the remainder to become a well-formed root of good nourishing food value. Upon arrival, Dad was informed of Oliver being absent due to a cold, and was asked to perform the milking of the cows. We proceeded to the barn to find the equipment is stored at the other end, so I followed Dad along the path between the stalls. Halfway down, Tom and Job, (the Shires) were in their stalls. Dad was a few yards ahead of me, and was past the stalls when Job lashed out with his hind legs, his hoofs coming very close to my face. A beam normally across the stall to prevent such a happening had not been replaced the day before. I have always given horses a fair margin since then.

But, as this was a day of crisis, Dad did well with the milking until he came to the last cow. A leg strap should have been applied before he commenced to milk, however, he sat on the stool and placed the pail, reached for the teats and WHUMP—the pail flew one way and Dad with stool went the other. Miss Woodcock had just stepped inside the door to witness the whole incident. She came instantly and gave capable assistance.

Labour unrest started in November 1926, but it seemed my father would not be involved, until the big blow came. Dad was called into the warden's office. He was told, "Due to the labour problems, your duties will now also include chauffeuring, and waiting at the dinner table." Father's reply came fast, with a flat refusal, "No! It's impossible to feed you *and* nurse you. I will pick up my cards." He meant that he could not provide the garden produce and do the extra duties the warden was requiring from him. So, he quit! It was late November 1926. Thus, his ties with St. Edward's School broken, his cricket days also came to an end. Douglas Bader continued at the school, and he became a prefect and captain of the first senior rugger team. He remained, gaining further recognition and advances, until he joined the Royal Air Force in September of 1928.

With Dad unemployed, the general strike in England began in November 1926. The Conservative Government was in power under Prime Minister Stanley Baldwin. It was his second term of office. Christmas Eve came, and with it a job for Dad at the Oxford Bus Company. It was total salvation for the family.

My family were staunch Conservatives, so strong in support that they were oblivious of the poor status. They considered themselves "middle-class", but my parents were almost penniless. It was my grandmother's belief that, "One must vote for those with money—only they can give you a fair standard of living." It has since become obvious to me that this was false.

Stanley Baldwin's Conservative Government brought in the Trade Disputes Act in 1927 to curtail the power of the labour unions. A disgusted nation elected a Labour government in 1929 under the leadership of Ramsay MacDonald. Meanwhile, in the United States, the stock market crashed, precipitating the depression of the 1930s, and greatly affecting Europe and the whole world.

As the strike progressed on into 1927, living became very difficult. Store shelves became almost bare. Fortunately for us, Dad had maintained a good garden of vegetables which spared us the pangs of hunger. Our biggest problem commenced in the late autumn when the days got shorter and cold. Coal was unobtainable since the merchants had locked it up for the duration of the strike. It remained that way until the strike ended. We still had wood left that Dad had received from St. Edward's School. Staff members were allowed some each year around Christmas- time, as a sort of bonus. We cut it sparingly, burning just enough to keep the dampness out of the house.

Thousands became unemployed. Unable to pay the rent, they were forced out into the street. It was a common sight while walking along, to see landlords stacking up the tenant's meager belongings on the pavements. This I witnessed in my hometown, the city of Oxford and the "seat of learning." Here the sons of the idle rich rubbed shoulders with the unfortunate ones, such as myself, who would never inherit a fortune or a comfortable income for the rest of our lives.

Mrs. Launchbury was one of several neighbours along Norreys Avenue who boarded men working at the various colleges that make up Oxford University. At the time, there were twenty-four colleges for male students, and three for women. There were only a token number of scholarships available, including Cecil Rhodes scholarships which were, (and still are) awarded to students around the world. The remaining students had their seats bought by parents, guardians, or donors.

About mid-December, 1926, a gentleman named Tom Marsland, who was seeking digs (room and board), was directed to my mother by Mrs. Launchbury. He was transferred from Manchester University to Oxford University Laboratories as a lab technician, to take up his duties in January 1927.

Dad's wages were no longer supporting us adequately, so Mum shifted the household around and took Mr. Marsland in. He settled down and became one of the family. As a hobby in the evenings, he built a good radio. He also became an officer of the 1st Oxford Boy's Brigade Company, and became a popular man in the community. We were now a family of six; a brother, Leonard had been born on August 31, 1927.

Tom loved swimming, and faithfully, every morning of the year, was up at 6:30 a.m. for a trip to the Long Bridges swimming place. This was a section in the backwater of the river Thames. He and a group of friends formed a Polar Bear Club. A punt was kept nearby in case of emergency, and in the winter when the ice was too thick, it was lifted out, leaving a hole for them to gain access to the water. This was replaced after the swim, maintaining the hole for the duration of the freeze-up.

During the summer months, I was taken along but due to the constant variation in the water's depth, I always shied off. When swimming became mandatory for scout camp, I then learned to swim at the Youlbury Scout Park pool, which was only waist deep. Here, I gained confidence, swam well, and lost my fear of water. I had qualified for my first scout camp, which was on a farm near Warwick Castle on the bank of the river Avon.

Our troop was comprised of four patrols, six boys each, with three leaders. Without delay, we were detailed to pitch the tents, ten in all. As it was already 3 p.m., it left us little time to complete the task before supper, so the large marquee, to be used jointly as a mess hall and for social functions, was first on the list. I assisted in digging the fire pit to put the kitchen area to work. The civilian cook made a great supper. It was fun to fill a palliasse with straw from the barn, roll up in the blankets, and sleep. Suddenly, I awoke in the early hours of the morning, and much to my surprise and horror, I had disgraced myself by wetting the bed.

After reveille and breakfast, the daily inspection layout of our personal kit for inspection was made. Since my blankets were hanging on a line, and not folded into my kit, the inspecting officer assessed a number of penalty points against our patrol. This meant we did not win the pennant awarded in competition for that day. It was a bad start for me, but before the week was over, this episode was overcome by trips to the Castle, and to other camps nearby for "Camp Fire" sing-song, following competitive games.

Our Scout Master became a vicar and took over a Parish Church near Liverpool. The troop, under a new leader, switched to Sea Scouts. I did not go with them, joining instead the 1st Oxford Boy's Brigade. Activities were many and varied, from the foot drill (for discipline), to gymnastics and physical training, band, first aid, wayfaring, and camping. Included also were seasonal sports and field competitions between other district companies or clubs.

I worked hard with the Boy's Brigade, gaining several certificates and badges. Our membership was large, being one hundred plus, ranging in age from twelve to seventeen. We were complete with a drum and fife, and bugle band, and I became a very good bugler.

Each year we camped at White Cliff Bay, a few miles south of Bembridge, on the Isle of Wight, a beautiful, small seaside resort, reached by a small-gauge, quaint looking train from Ryde. After an overnight train trip from Oxford to Portsmouth, we would board the large paddle steamer to cross the Solent, taking about twenty minutes.

It was the same stretch of the English Channel where the historic ship, *The Mary Rose*, foundered in the 15th century. From the camp-site, we could see the famous ocean- going liners pass by, going to all corners of the globe. It was the only route in and out of Southhampton; the western approach was impossible due to the famous tourist attractions, "The Needles", and "Dolphin Sand", barring access. I can recall seeing such vessels of the Cunard Line as the *Aquitania, Berengaria*, and *Queen Mary,* and White Star Line's, *Majestic.* There were also the Orient Pacific Line's, *Strathcona Castle*, and *Strathmore Castle;* the German ships, *Europa*, and *Bremen*; the French Ship, *Ile de France;* and the Italian ship, *Rex.* They all had pleasing lines and characteristics by which they could be easily identified.

The years I spent with both organizations proved invaluable to me in later life. The Boy's Brigade celebrated its 50th anniversary in Wembley Stadium, London, in 1933. I was in attendance to represent the 1st Oxford Company. I still fail to see why Baden Powell, a great friend of our founder, William Smith, broke away to form the Boy Scouts.

In 1928, I became a choir boy at St. Lawrence Church in South Hinksey, where my father was singing tenor. The church was built in the 11th century by the Normans, and was complete with the usual square tower, which held four bells. They could not be rung, as the tenor bell had been stolen.

The Boy's Brigade was a part of St. Matthews Church, and after my voice changed, I became a tenor and joined the choir. Marjorie (who later became my wife) and I later became members of the West Oxford Choral Society, taking part in four renditions of the Messiah at the Oxford City Hall.

# 3

—

## *Fall Fair, University Sports Activities & Splitting the Atom*

After an unusually hot, five-week summer holiday, the St. Giles Fair in Oxford nicely rounded off our vacation and ushered in the new school year. There were all types of roundabouts, from "Nicholl's" horses and chair planes, to "Bird's" and "Thurston's" cars. There were also whirlers, cakewalk, dodger cars, and American swing-boats, which threatened to break free of their moorings and fly into the bedrooms of adjacent houses. "Housey, housey", the "coconut shies," (where Mr. Marsland won several coconuts), and skittles, were games to test your throwing power. Your strength could be demonstrated by swinging the sledgehammer hard enough to send the gauge-weight up the pole, to ring a bell at the top.

There were also numerous sideshows and fortunetellers. For a sixpence, I finally persuaded one fortuneteller to forecast a future for my friend, Maurice Coles, and myself. She took us into her little tent where we sat on chairs, facing a small table. It was cloth covered, with a large crystal ball standing in the centre. The gypsy stood on the other side, leant over, and peered at us very closely with large, dark eyes, then sat down. Maurice was going to have a fairly quiet life; he would not be an active man, but one working with and reading books for the press.

When she turned to me, I saw a total change of expression in her face; it became serious, frowning, and then wrinkles formed in her forehead, down the side of her cheeks and into her lips. Then, she spoke in a much deeper, resonant voice, "I see so much about you, and you are too young for me to tell you all, but you will be widely traveled, under unforeseen circumstances. Now go, and give me time to compose myself." As we left, expressing our thanks, she did appear deeply distressed.

It was approaching the third anniversary of Tom Marsland coming to live with us. On a frosty evening, we all sat down to dinner, and Tom related to us that it had been a day of history making within the Oxford Laboratories. To quote: "Today, seventeen scientists split the atom! This can now be used for industrial purposes, medical purposes, or destruction."

Stanley Baldwin and his Conservatives were given a golden opportunity to pursue this further, develop the A-bomb and avert World War II. Instead, they sat and argued over the strengthening of various strategic points around the world, and did nothing.

I enjoyed the elementary classes at the Boys School. I achieved good marks and was considered a good prospect for a higher education, which would follow after writing the scholarship entrance exams—one year away.

Spring arrived, and with it, the old, traditional boat race between the arch-rivals, Oxford and Cambridge Universities. In May, each of the Oxford colleges races their eights crews. The boats have eight rowers and a cox (coxswain). Rowers are chosen for their physical stature, strength, and rowing capabilities. Five races were, and still are, held each day for one week, known as Eights Week.

That stretch of the River Thames, between Folly Bridge to the west and Iffley Lock to the east, is known as the Isis. Each college maintained a beautifully decorated barge on the river, as its boat station. The boats line up (line astern); two boat-lengths apart, at the east end of the Isis, the last boat just west of Iffley Lock. The first boat to cross the finish line (close to Folly Bridge), after the 6 p.m. race, claimed the title "Head of the river."

At the sound of the starting gun, the boats strike out hoping to catch up with, and bump the boat ahead. If a boat is successful in bumping, it takes over the position of the bumped boat at the start of the next race (of that division), on the following day. I can recall top honours being won frequently by Brasenose, Oriel, Magdalen, and Corpus Christi colleges. The cox of each boat added a lot of colour, wearing a striking blazer, cap, neck scarf, and gloves. His elaborate outfit was made complete with a number of flowers tucked inside the scarf and jacket front; for example, Magdalen might use three huge, red peonies, and Brasenose, three superb Madonna Lilies.

We finished school each day about 4:15 in the afternoon, and several of us would rush down to the river to watch the last two races. Spectators of all ages were there in the thousands, standing or squatting close to the riverbank. This was necessary; otherwise, you would be trampled by the hordes of supporters for each crew, who raced along the pathway, wearing scarves in their college colours. They shouted themselves hoarse and brandished small pistols, firing live ammunition over or between the spectators as they went. They hoped the bullets would strike the oars of the opposing rowers, disrupting their strokes and enabling their own crew to bump the boat ahead.

With the rowing, Oxford would also welcome the D'Oyly Carte Opera Company. This entertainment and excitement would lead us into summer and the cricket season. The Oxford University team was chosen from the Oxford colleges' best players in rugby football, soccer, cricket, and field hockey. When the cricket team was playing at home, Stan Long and I would be off to the park the moment we were out of school. We would catch the bus for a one-penny ride to South Park, then dash for a spot on the turf to watch the last two hours of play.

Invariably, we would sit by a very smartly dressed gentleman in gray tweeds with matching trilby hat. His striking appearance was enhanced by a well-groomed, salt and pepper Van Dyck beard. He carried a walking stick with a hooped handle, which opened into a seat. This he placed to one side, then sprawled out with us on the beautiful grass. He was not alone; his companion was a magnificent, red King Charles spaniel (I have never seen a larger or finer specimen of this breed), and we all became good friends.

The famous county cricketers on the visiting teams were the big attraction of varsity games. Many of them had won their caps playing for England in the test matches. The "visitors" represented the various counties of England, or were one of the Commonwealth teams touring England for the test matches. These included Australia, India, West Indies, and South Africa. They visited, alternately, on a two to three year schedule.

This was great entertainment, and it was free; there were no gate charges into the park. We spent many hours watching the formidable batting of many great batsmen. Of the county men, Sutcliffe, Leyland, Hammond, Woolley, Paynter and Jardine, were outstanding examples. Australia's Bradman and McNab, also Nawab of Pataudi, and Dulepsinghy of India, were stars of the touring teams. Even with all the "centuries" (100 runs) these men scored, they certainly did not have it all their own way. There were also many great bowlers who could flatten the wickets in short order. Verity was a distinguished slow bowler. Bowes and the controversial Larwood with his body line bowling, were deadly fast bowlers. Others were excellent spin bowlers: Fender from Kent, and O'Reilly of Australia.

One of the finest cricketers, in my opinion, was Les Ames of Kent, an exceptional wicketkeeper and batter. Stan and I enjoyed the performances of such cricket "greats," and occasionally we were able to collect an autograph; these were special hours which I will never forget.

# 4

—

## *Mixed Classrooms & Lawrence of Arabia*

In August of 1930, Tom Marsland married a schoolteacher, Jean McNeal, from Moss Side, Manchester. They bought a good house at 28 St. Omer Road in Oxford.

We returned to school and discovered that the boy's domain was lost forever. The classes were mixed; our desk partners were girls! It soon became obvious that in these early years, the girls were ahead of us. We boys found some relief from the task of trying to catch up during our half-days at the woodworking centre, and on Friday afternoons, playing various sports (soccer and cricket). I enjoyed personal achievement in running, obtaining excellent times in quarter mile, one mile, and cross-country.

Difficulties arose for both teachers and boys. Continuity was needed for the girls, whereas the boys were still struggling to get a handle on the topic, which was ahead of our schedule and above our heads. The day the exams were written, many of us could not understand the terminology of the question, let alone write an answer. Several of the boys failed, including me.

During the last two years in school, I became a good distance runner, going on to represent the Boy's Brigade in competition with other clubs. My running was consistent, and I won many good races with outstanding times. At various training meets, there would be approximately twenty of us running with several of the boys' mothers turning out to watch our progress. My mother, after much persuasion from the others, finally decided to attend a meet. We got off to a good start on a four and a half-mile run. At about the two-mile mark, I pulled up lame with a stabbing pain in my right knee. I never ran again, so my mother never did see me cross the finish line.

Monday morning, December 1, 1931, Douglas Bader crashed his plane, a "Bulldog," doing some ridiculous aerobatics upon take off. He lost his right leg during the late afternoon, and within forty-eight hours, the left leg was also removed. Bader made a miraculous recovery considering his chances were very slim. He remained with the Air Force until he was mobile again, on tin legs. He was discharged and found work with the Shell Oil Company, but he never lost his desire to fly.

The last day of school before the Christmas break (1933) closed with a social evening for the students who were leaving. During the past two months, officials of the Employment Exchange had placed most of us into some type of work. Over refreshments, we discussed old times and exchanged opinions with our teachers and classmates. We held high hopes for a bright future. I was one of a few yet to find employment, although it had been suggested I go into woodworking. In my mind, I wanted work that would demand my whole interest and offer good incentives. My ability to work with wood was excellent, but the wages were poor. At the time, I was reaching beyond my capabilities, but it did not deter future ambitions.

February 14, 1934, I started work at the Alden Press Oxford Ltd., where I was assigned diversified duties. The first hour I would spend bailing wastepaper (trimmings from the bindery) and cleaning. I then would deliver printed material around the city, plus any galleys of type required by a jobbing shop in town. The balance of my time was spent assisting with the packing of flat-sheet goods of books being sent to London for binding and publication. The work was heavy, and as I progressed, my wages were increased every six months. Gradually, I learned the various types and qualities of paper, with their names and sizes. I was taught to operate the guillotine, cutting paper as required for the smaller machines, and warehouse and stocktaking duties. My job required that I attend night school classes in layout design. I also continued woodwork classes in furniture making techniques. My teacher, Mr. Lay of Summertown, worked with the Oxford School Board for many years. He was a well-respected and talented man.

During this time, my great-aunt, Jane Bolton, came to Oxford and took up residence with Mrs. Hogarth as a lady's companion. It was during one of my visits with her that I met Lawrence of Arabia, who was a close family friend of the Hogarths. He had been with Mr. Hogarth (an archaeologist) in Palestine, but now Mr. Hogarth was curator of the Ashmolean Museum in Oxford. Lawrence would stand his straight flat-tank Royal Enfield motorcycle against the old, iron railings just in front of the sitting room window at 39A St. Giles. I am positive he was there the night before the accident that killed him in 1935.

Approximately one year later, Jonathan Cape of Bedford Square, London, received the rights to publish Lawrence's account of his Arabian adventures, the "Seven Pillars of Wisdom." The Alden Press received the honour of printing it. We started out with five thousand copies (deluxe edition) at five guineas each, followed by hundreds of thousands at one pound, ten shillings each (700 pages crown quarto, 7½" x 10".)

I spoke of this with Mrs. Hogarth, and she revealed to me that Lawrence had made a private publication for his family and friends, of one hundred copies (1926). She showed me her copy, producing it from a locked, steel case. It was bound in solid leather covers, approximately a quarter inch thick, printed on heavy paper with several coloured pictures (watercolors or pastel), drawn by Lawrence himself. Mrs. Hogarth valued it at 700 pounds.

At the print shop, we were busy and most days I worked overtime. I had reached that period in my life when I required more money. Growing up meant new clothes, another bicycle (my mode of conveyance to work), but more importantly, I now had a fiancée, Marjorie Mills. We enjoyed a good movie or the theatre, especially the opera when the Sadler Wells or Carl Rosa Opera Company came to Oxford. We spent many hours playing chess, waiting for the doors to open for a Gilbert and Sullivan presentation by the D'Oyly Carte Company.

I had become a very busy young man and found myself overextended. The Boys Brigade had given me a good start into manhood. The night school classes in layout design fell apart due to a sick teacher, so I dropped both activities in 1936. I continued with woodworking, which I was determined to keep as my hobby and not my line of endeavour.

The Oxford Waterworks reservoir was very close to home, and was comprised of two lakes. The water level was maintained by an inlet pipe, which brought the water down from the Thames River, north of Oxford—about four miles away. It was good and clean with lots of fish, and we would sneak in along the railway bank to fish. During freeze up, ice skaters did likewise. This was a very dangerous practice because the water was being continuously pumped a further four miles eastward into a tower which was at a higher elevation. The water, gravity fed into the distribution system, gave a household about thirty pounds of pressure in the taps. The constant movement of water under the ice would create cracks, and between 1927 and 1939 there were several fatalities. The skaters would vanish, and it took several days before their bodies were recovered.

A new reservoir was built west of Oxford, using water from the river Windrush, which took five years to fill. It replaced the lakes near home, and the filter beds and cooling pond became swimming pools and model-boat sailing areas. The lakes were opened for legal fishing (with a licence), and for boats with sail or manual propulsion.

A very hot summer (1937 I believe), created a catastrophe of unbelievable proportions. The river Thames became so low that the lake levels could not be maintained. One Sunday morning, the water surface was a mass of dead fish: bream, carp, tench, barbel, and pike. They were very large, but we never knew they were there. After clean up, the officials estimated eight tons of dead fish. The largest fish I ever saw caught was by Mr. Kent of Lake Street. He carried it to Haines (the Fish & Chip Shop) to weigh it, and it turned the scales to twenty-six and a half pounds. It was caught by spinning, on a six-inch chrome spoon.

# 5

—

## *Mobilization*

It seemed the Alden Press could not get copies of "The Seven Pillars of Wisdom" into the marketplace fast enough. Wherever one turned, prosperity was evident, yet there were still those desperate for a square meal and a roof over their heads.

In Germany, Hitler was trying every conceivable way to restore his country to a strong, international power. Their economy was so poor that he ordered cigarette butts saved, broken open and the contents re-rolled to conserve tobacco. His Youth movement increased every day. They turned against their parents, families and friends to pursue their quest for power. Horror stories reached England in a continuous stream, and the persecution of Jews in London began, close to my grandmother's home. Their storefronts were smeared with paint in the shape of swastikas. It was through such discrimination that Hitler gained tremendous power over Germany.

Hitler moved quickly into the neutral zone between France and Germany, known as the Saar Territory. This zone had been established at the signing of the Treaty of Versailles in 1919, following World War I. The world watched without comment. Another move was made in March 1938, the invasion of Czechoslovakia. It was this action that created a sense of urgency for my friends and me to finalize our decisions to join one of the military services.

At the print shop, fourteen of us were eligible for immediate conscription if hostilities broke out. Mickey Barney, a territorial and staff sergeant in an anti-tank regiment, suggested we make a choice instead of waiting to be called up and placed. So most of us went with him to the 4th Oxford Infantry barracks to enlist. We signed up on a temporary basis until a new division might be formed. Warner, Bradfield and I, realizing it could be some time before a decision was made, decided to try the Royal Air Force, and proceeded to Harburton House, Headington, Oxford.

On June 1, 1939, my sister's birthday, I stood before Squadron Leader Keene and swore allegiance to King and country. In return, he gave me my enlisted number—750280. My part-time training as an equipment assistant started immediately, two nights a week at Upper Heyford aerodrome. It was a great thrill to see so many young men, from all walks of life, congregate on the railroad platforms and proceed to their various training units. Our group required two railroad coaches, which were added to the Oxford and Birmingham Express. This created much confusion on Mondays and Thursdays for the railroad officials, because Heyford meant an extra stop, and delay of the train's arrival in Birmingham.

When returning to Oxford, the truck transport between the aerodrome and the station was hazardous and erratic. We all stood up, clinging to whatever we could reach: a leather thong or the metal strappings attached to the cover frame, to maintain our balance as the truck sped and swerved along the country lanes. Invariably, the train had already arrived and was waiting for us. The guard was pulling out his hair, waving his lantern, and shrieking at us as we tumbled from the transports and rushed to the coaches. Once seated, each would take stock of his personal damage: a twisted ankle, bruises of arms or legs, and abrasions of hands or kneecaps. These injuries happened when we all tried to clamber over the tailgate of the truck at the same time, with many falling due to the height of the drop to the ground.

Due to the urgent need for tradesmen, each man was assigned to the task considered closest to his civilian occupation. We were completely outfitted within the month. The so-called square-bashing (marching and rifle handling) and other bullshit was put aside. War clouds hung heavy; the anticipated move by Hitler to attack Poland had become inevitable. It was a waiting game; tension was felt by everyone.

The call for instant mobilization was announced early in the afternoon on Friday, September 1. The fourteen of us in the printing works congregated outside the president's office. H. J. and his brother, Raymond Alden, bade us farewell, and promised that our jobs would be there when we returned. With a handshake from our fellow workers, we went to report to our respective headquarters.

By the time I reached Harburton House, it was swarming and reeling under the number who had arrived. The allocating of postings was a slow process. Each airman required a service book, rail pass and posting form, which could only be completed after the designated aerodrome was known. The afternoon dragged on into evening; it was a long get-acquainted hour, over a pint of good brew. I was posted to #2 Flying Training School, at Brize Norton, approximately thirty miles from home. Little time was left for me to put personal business in order and reach the railroad station in time for the 10:00 a.m. train leaving from Oxford the following morning.

Mr. Hearne arrived at the house with his taxi, in good time. With a lump in my throat, I kissed my mother, father, two sisters, and brother goodbye. My next door neighbour, Mr. Spencer, served in the Royal Army Flying Corps. He had worked, in conjunction with Lawrence of Arabia, in Palestine during World War I. He handed me his flying corps belt to wear for good luck, and with his wife, bade me farewell. Fifteen minutes later, I presented a railroad pass for a one way ticket, entered the station platform, and headed for a group of fellows standing by the train. In turn, I was greeted by some of those who had made our weekly trips to Heyford, and received a friendly acknowledgment from the remainder. We were a small contingent of about thirty, trying to be jovial, but somewhat subdued by the prospects of what lay ahead. The general consensus was "It's going to be a long time before we are back in civvy street."

This little train, similar to those one finds in a fairy tale picture book, was pulled by a series 0-6-0 locomotive, named "Fair Rosamund". It puffed, chugged, and snorted its way along a single track, away from the main line. We passed through little stations I never knew existed, until we reached our destination of Bampton, which was on the south side of the flying field. After a long wait for motor transport, we finally circumnavigated the field to the main-gate entrance. We were housed in the old wooden huts that had been used during the building of the new aerodrome.

Within the hour, our contingent was on parade and headed to the "Anti-Gas" station. We received a respirator and specified protective clothing in case of gas attacks. These were carried at all times, the clothing rolled tightly and attached to the respirator case. A respirator was also issued to every man, woman and child, the civilian type if they were not enrolled in one of the services, Home Guard or Red Cross.

We went to the bedding quarters for sheets and blankets. Back in the hut, we fired the wood and coal-burning stove, to take away the chill caused by the dampness within the hut. After the evening meal, we received the password for the day and signed the passbook at the guardhouse.

Approximately two miles north of the main gate stood the "Bee Hive," a large pub at the Carterton crossroads, where we spent the evening. It was here that I became acquainted with several service men, who were to become my buddies. At one time or another, we had all played the popular game of darts, and before you could settle comfortably into a seat, someone would be challenging you to a game. If you were slow at figures, cheating would put you on the paying end of a losing game. However, keeping one eye on the scoreboard and throwing a respectable dart would place an extra drink at your elbow. I could not drink a lot and frequently abstained, arriving back at the billet to enjoy a good night's sleep.

The next morning being Sunday, reveille was not sounded and we could remain in bed. However, half a dozen of us were up, shaved, dressed, and headed for the compound cookhouse. Here we found the cooking staff of the women's army corps who had also arrived the day before. This would turn out to be the one breakfast never forgotten. As we arrived at the service counter in the mess hall, a tall blonde asked if we would like eggs and bacon, and if so, how many eggs. She would pass our request along to the other girls who then proceeded to cook while we stood waiting. This line up became very long, and the girl's faces were now all highly coloured crimson, as they struggled to get sufficient food cooked. Eventually, we were served, and I must admit we all ate a scrumptious breakfast. This routine was quickly changed when the mess sergeant heard about it.

Christmas 1939 arrived with a deep freeze setting in across Northern Europe. Leave was given to the men according to their religious faith. Since I was an Anglican on leave, it was my duty to be back in camp for guard detail on December 31. The station was short of personnel and tradesmen were required to take their turn. The night was bitterly cold, and my post was at the main gate. The New Year came in, along with the last busload of men back from leave. Those of other faiths now started their leave, as the ice was building up on the telephone wires. By 2:00 a.m. on New Year's Day, the ice measured two inches thick on the wires, and with the weight of some two dozen lines, the poles began to break. Each pole snapped with a resounding crack, like that of rifle-fire, and for fifteen miles they crashed to the ground. There was mass chaos across England; the difficulties we endured! The terrible weather enabled the factories to build arms, tanks and aircraft, free of interruption from bombing raids. Two weeks passed before enemy aircraft appeared again over England. The French, with the British Expeditionary Force, came under attack after Norway and Denmark had succumbed on May 10, 1940. The Germans attacked Belgium by swinging around the Maginot Line with airborne troops. From there, they came westward against the allies, driving them towards the Channel. The British units gradually lost ground. They entered Dunkirk, and behind a last line of defence, withdrew to the beaches. The soldiers were picked up by thousands of small boats, and were either ferried to larger vessels or brought home directly. The Alden Press group had lost three or four men, including Staff Sergeant Barney. The bed sheets we had received upon arrival were collected and sent to the Radcliffe Infirmary, Oxford, to be used for bandages. There were many casualties.

A lone raider flew in from the north, aiming its last bomb at the water tower; it missed, blowing up a parked staff-car at the base of the tower. This marked the first attack on Brize Norton.

The main stores received a new officer squadron leader, McLaughlin, brother of Victor McLaughlin, the renowned Hollywood actor in the United States. When he surveyed the station defences, compared to the size of our complex, it left him speechless. Army units were moving in with heavy anti-aircraft guns, and facilities to accommodate them were being installed. The squadron leader made three or four trips to Air Ministry to discuss our plight, and before he left the station, there were some additions for defence.

We now had three Spitfires stationed at #6 Maintenance Unit, on the far side of the aerodrome, for air protection. For defence against possible paratroop landings, one antiquated "armadillo" (a relic from the early stages of World War I, 1914) was acquired and placed at one corner of the field, like a monument.

# 6

—

## *Attack on Brize Norton*

By August 16, 1940, the Battle of Britain had attained its maximum height, with Goering, the Nazi Air Marshall, acting upon Hitler's demands to crush London. Hitler believed that, "To devastate London is to demoralize and defeat the British people." It was on this day that the Luftwaffe attacked aerodromes, destroying fighter planes, and paved the way for an all-out assault on British towns and cities.

Only three months previously, the R.A.F. fighter strength had been reduced by one-third during the attempt to take over in the air while convoying the British Expeditionary Force back from Dunkirk. By now, the strain of many hours on duty was showing among the pilots of the defensive units. However, the situation could have been much worse, if not hopelessly lost, had radar not been available as a watchdog to track down the raiders and assist in directing the fighters into the attack. This enabled the pilots to obtain more rest, and reduced the scouting for enemy raiders by physical means.

I was a storekeeper with No.2 R.A.F. Advanced Flying Training School at Brize Norton, situated near Witney and some twenty miles northwest of Oxford. It was on this same day (August 16, 1940) that I came under enemy fire for the first time. This target, most valuable to the Royal Air Force because of its potential pilot replacement program, meant only one thing to the enemy—destroy it now, or be destroyed later by those receiving their final training. The more damaging the blow on such a vital facility, the less likelihood of a sixty-pupil class passing on to breach the gaps in our defence.

After a normal day's work in the store, I was one of two men to remain at the post for night duty. Responsibility rested heavily on the men who were detailed for late duties each day. Fate deemed this evening to be extraordinary, with both flight courses, (Squadrons A & B) in operation, and heavy supplies coming in from distant maintenance units.

Five road tankers containing high-octane gasoline arrived. This called for immediate duty at the pumps to eliminate the hazard before nightfall. In order to attend to this task, I relieved myself from duty in mainstores and proceeded to the storage tanks (six 12,000-gallon tanks). There at the dump, delivery was made to a selected tank (either 100 or 90 octane) after the correct cocks had been opened between intake pipe, screening chamber, pump, and tank. Each road tanker had five compartments. To the storage-tank intake pipe, I attached ten hoses: one to each compartment of two of the tankers. Before pumping could commence, a dipstick reading of each compartment had to be recorded, as well as the reading of each storage tank receiving the new supply. Temperature readings were necessary to determine the exact amount delivered because gas varies three gallons per thousand gallons for each degree of temperature (up or down) from the mean temperature of sixty degrees.

At 5:50 p.m., I had the pump running and was taking in from the first pair of tankers, at the south side of the tanks. On the north side, I had coupled two bowsers, used to service the planes with fuel. It was a beautiful, English summer sky with no clouds, and wherever you looked, at all points of the compass you could see training planes flying.

Suddenly, the first bowser operator, pointing to the sky, said to me, "Surely those two planes at seven o'clock (Southwest) coming in the sun, are not Oxford's?"

"No!" was my reply. "They're Junkers 88's."

Here were two enemy planes flying with our trainers at 1600 feet, taking up bombing positions while the two of us stood watching, helpless because we were not located at a focal point to raise an alarm.

Junkers 88's!!! Suddenly, as our words registered in our minds, the bomb bay doors swung open. A stick of ten bombs stood out beneath the silhouette of each plane. There was no time to panic because the inevitable had happened. I dashed to the switch panel and pulled the master lever, stopping all pumps. The shelters were our only thought, but at a gas pump, they do not install such things. So, here we were, two human beings running like scared rabbits from their burrows, doing our utmost to put as much distance between us and the storage tanks as was humanly possible.

Now we could hear screeching whistles as the bombs were zooming towards the earth so fast that the human eye could not see them. As the first one struck, with a resounding explosion, I hit the grass flat on my face. Then followed a series of explosions as each bomb found its mark. Suddenly, something brushed my hair and struck the ground with a soft thud. As I raised my head in the stillness that followed, I discovered a piece of shrapnel in the turf. It had singed my hair! I was doubly lucky considering I had not retrieved my helmet from the pump house. Questions arose within me: was I blessed with nine lives? Had the first one just been lost? At least I figured that my number had been on it, but it had missed. Finally, it was cool enough to handle. I plucked it from its alien resting-place and carried it away as a souvenir.

There was something unusual about this operation. Then it occurred to me that from the entire ground defence units surrounding the aerodrome, not a single muzzle had puffed fire. The junior store officer was duty officer-of-the-day when the attack started. He was fulfilling his duties, inspecting fortified positions. The army manned 3.7-inch antiaircraft guns, and was waiting for the order to fire. The duty officer's truck was armed with a Lewis machine-gun, and he was carrying a revolver. A tragedy of serious proportion—he had failed to pick up ammunition and could not fire the warning shot to open fire.

On standing up, it was evident that the bombardiers had laid perfect patterns. One stick of bombs had registered hits on two planes sitting on the tarmac, a hangar, one corner of the main stores, the side of the powerhouse, a barrack block, the rear side of the cook house, the ration stores, and a house in the married quarters.

The bomb that hit the powerhouse blew the head off the driver of the first gas tanker. It was picked up some ten to fifteen feet away from the torso. This gory mess was all that remained of a young family man from Gloucester who had misjudged the direction of the planes before he started to vacate the pump area.

There was one other killed and twenty-seven hospitalized, four with serious injuries. Most of them were strafed by the plane's tail gunners as they mounted guard on the barrack square.

The material losses were high. Additionally, there were thirty-seven planes and a second hangar destroyed by the second stick of bombs. Most of the planes destroyed were in the hangars being serviced on various maintenance inspections. By nightfall, the first big aerial plunge at Britain had been completed, with heavy losses to both sides.

In early September, I was transferred to "A" Squadron flight stores and an insurmountable task. A decision had been made to train pilots for twin engine aircraft only, leaving me responsible for all equipment held for Harvard single engine aircraft to be dispatched to Oddicombe. The paper work was overwhelming—every article recorded by part number and removed from squadron tallies.

All aircraft lost in the Air Raid were being replaced by "Airspeed Oxford's", delivered by a ferry crew service. One morning the aerodrome was socked in by fog, closing down all flying. I met one of the ferry pilots for Air Transport Auxiliary, Mrs. Amy Johnson, who prior to the war had become a prominent flyer, winning several international flight competitions between England and Australia. Later she married the renowned Jim Mollison who had also become famous with his flying achievement. At 10:00 a.m. that particular morning we were chatting by her Gypsy Moth, which she had brought in the night before, but she was unable to leave as planned. To my knowledge, there was no further flying that day. On January 5, 1941, whilst on a delivery, she crashed into the Thames estuary and lost her life.

# 7

—

## *Posting to #242 Squadron, Embarkation & Treacherous Seas*

Leave was restored after a two-week cancellation, a lull in attacks being evident, and it lasted two weeks. It was felt, and often suggested, that I moved with a guardian angel, because the lull and resumed leave coincided with my wedding plans. The wedding took place at St. Matthews on August 24, 1940, and Marjorie and I established residence at her parent's home in Oxford. The ensuing six months, not realized at the time, were to be the greatest and happiest days of our married life. Only when on our honeymoon in Devon, did the real meaning of war strike home to me. Deep inside I felt that these circumstances were to be a very painful process to many men, wives and their families during the bitter days that lay ahead.

Easter of 1941 was three days away when the biggest blow came to both of us, the loss of my wife's mother, a petite woman with a wonderful personality who had gained the love and affection of the whole community.

Two further air raids were encountered at the aerodrome before marching orders were received for me to report to my first operational unit, 242 Hurricane Fighter Squadron. Such a posting each man in the forces must expect from time to time. However, with this transfer came the inevitable embarkation to an unknown destination.

Owing to the urgency of this movement, leave was restricted to five days (120 hours) before a parting of unknown duration was to commence. The question immediately arose, how could Marjorie and I make the most of so short a period? Of course, the solution was quite simple; take the old jaunts adjacent to home, reminisce awhile, and relive a few of those wonderful moments which first brought us together.

We thought of our visits to the theatre and the way Oxford welcomed the D'Oyly Carte Opera Company. They performed the ever-popular Gilbert and Sullivan operas over a three-week period with an excellent repertoire. We heard outstanding performances by Sidney Granville, Martyn Green, Dorothy Gill, Muriel Dickson, and Derek Oldham, under the baton of Isidore Godfrey. Days later, everyone would be swinging along to the tunes from "Mikado", "Gondoliers", "Pirates of Penzance", and others. We spoke of our friends in Devon and the hikes we took on the Moors, and of the lunch baskets packed with delicious pears and clotted cream.

Then there was our dream, the house we hoped to build. We had already drawn plans of rooms, furnishings and location; there was a lot to think about. Here, in this way, we would remember each other a little better and realize just how much responsibility we had to remain alive.

To keep in constant touch and telling of our love would be impossible, but we could look into the future optimistically, hoping that such a parting would be brief and not exist too long. In this sense, one can feel the measure of security that is so essential to each other for a successful marriage.

There were just two of us leaving Brize Norton on this posting, and our destination was Manston, a fighter-based aerodrome on the southeast corner of England. Enroute, we traversed London, Paddington to Victoria, where we met with others heading to the same destination.

We arrived to find the barrack blocks badly damaged, which meant a transfer into private housing a few miles away. At the same time, we learned that 242 Hurricane Squadron had completed its tour of duty and was now in North Wales. Four days later, additional personnel had assembled, and we filled a complete train and left under the cover of darkness to join forces. At a London station, we stopped and ate at a very good service canteen; this was operated by a voluntary group of elite ladies who were compassionate and kind. The train continued northward only to be held in a tunnel until the enemy had completed its mission. We continued on to Anglesey Island, across the Menai Bridge from Bangor, North Wales.

Here 242 Squadron assembled to prepare for embarkation. Beyond any shadow of doubt, this was welcome news for the Germans, as the most formidable barrier to their attack had been removed from the strategic position of southeast England. Most of the boys were Canadians, who had fought their way back from the defence of Dunkirk, and later were commended for the magnificent work that they had performed. Upon reforming, they came under the leadership of Wing Commander Bader, by this time a POW in France. These men of 242 had warmed to the ideals of their aggressive wing commander, whose determination to exterminate these barbaric intruders made them reluctant to move on.

The storekeepers were faced with inconceivable difficulties, due to the necessary checking and packing of every requisite for both men and planes. Each tool kit—there were nine types, comprised of many assorted tools to enable fitters, riggers, electricians, and radio men to work efficiently, plus there were lesser kits for the mates of each trade. Clothing parades were staged to equip each man with both tropical and arctic clothing, as the destination of this particular posting was not divulged.

This task absorbed the better part of six weeks due to poor distribution, or the lack of certain items. However, when all was complete and crated up, approximately forty shipping tons (40 cubic feet per ton) were ready for the boat. Squadron stores now had all necessary aerodrome equipment, which included such navigational aids as control lights and runway flares, radio parts and signal apparatus, tool kits plus spares, and barrack and cookhouse needs. In other boats, there were fifty Hurricane fighters, ammunition, and seventeen assorted pieces of trucking transport, including a gas bowser; this rounded off the squadron as a fully self-supporting mobile unit.

Relaxation was now first in the storekeepers' minds. A trip to the much spoken of "Castle Hotel" drinking room in Bangor was considered the right thing to do, being this was their first trip to this small university town of North Wales. So here in a room lavishly furnished with antiques, in silverware and pewter steins, I was initiated into the 242 Hurricane Fighter Squadron. Each and every man was proud to serve in this unit because of its undaunting successes whenever it had made contact with the enemy.

Its achievement had gained the fullest respect of the Luftwaffe, and of the men themselves. Determination had arisen that no foe could possibly clip the squadron's wings. So, with this spirit, 242 left North Wales for the embarkation port of Greenoch, Scotland, leaving behind (for all these hospitable Welsh people) two songs, smutty as they were, but still with the essence of true comradeship between men who really were, beyond all doubt, the finest fighter squadron of the Royal Air Force at that time. They sang with all their hearts, "We are the evils of the night, who would rather … than fight. Good old 242," and secondly, "Hold my hand in the blackout, Mother, Night is coming on, and I'm far away from home sweet home."

The *Empress of Australia* was anchored out in midstream, and soon the tender was cast off to ply its way to the port side of this beautiful ship with the most pleasing lines. She was a magnificent feat of engineering, designed and built in Germany as a steam yacht for the ex-Kaiser, and taken over by Britain when reparations were being paid after the First World War. She had a displacement tonnage of 21,500 tons. Her main deck (promenade), circumnavigated on foot measured one-eighth of a mile and was approximately sixty feet above the Plimsoll line.

The entrance hall, situated amidships, called for everyone to mount the bridge deck of the tender. This caused much consternation among the men, for each man was required to carry his full backpack, as well as gas respiration equipment and gas clothing, a steel helmet, a rifle, and two kit bags. At the same time, you had to be a contortionist to gain the next deck up by climbing the narrow stairwells and then the gangplank, which was continuously varying its elevation due to the swell of the water rocking the boats.

All who entered the ship were amazed by the welcome they received from the steward, clad in a smartly starched white suit, handing out berth and dining cards and instructions on how to proceed to the assigned part within the ship's bowels. Here, for a few moments, my pals and I were treated like normal civilians embarking on a world cruise, respected for whom we were. However, to our disapproval, we soon found ourselves at water level on the port side (left), standing in what was meant to serve as a mess hall (but it never did, since we were to hang hammocks and convert this space into living quarters). Stowing essential equipment for the journey where it would leave a passage way across the deck, we dropped the balance into a locker room another two decks down. A similar area on the starboard side served for the same purpose. In these two sections, the 242 Squadron, with strangely enough two hundred and forty-two personnel (less the senior NCOs, Sergeants and up), was confined.

All available cabin space on lower decks had been taken over by army personnel (including the whole deck beneath sea level), with shared ablution and allocated rest areas. The remaining two-thirds of the ship was for the sparse number of officers and senior NCOs. Here it must be emphasized, that this (and all other troop ships, especially the *Andes)* was an utter disgrace to the British War Office. For nine weeks at sea the men lived like rats, huddled up in the steerage section of these boats. If a torpedo had struck, thousands would have been lost for lack of lifeboats and rafts. Although every man had his life jacket, would this have sufficed while fighting panic? No! The psychological effect of being with a large number of people suddenly trying to emerge from a series of staircases, between the watertight compartments of the ship's hull, would merely contribute to a catastrophe. In my estimation, human wedges would have formed on the staircases, and all would have been lost. In addition, section leaders, being so divided, would have been unable to get close enough to direct evacuation.

At 10:00 p.m. on December 8, 1941, this beautiful boat, in the competent hands of the Canadian Pacific Railway, weighed anchor. With her, other liners and cargo vessels started to slip secretly away into the blackness beyond. This movement of ships was in complete keeping with the local inhabitants of the Castle Hotel; they had said that the largest convoy ever to leave England in this war was to be on the night of December 8, 1941.

With my buddies, I stood at the guardrail in the moonlight, looking first to the east, for here was a scene that would live with us forever. The moon was at the third quarter, illuminating the two mountain peaks just beneath her. The shore where we had stood earlier that day was now so efficiently blacked out that there were neither reflections nor visible lights. Then our small group, after moments of meditation, turned to peer into the direction the ship was moving, to find just a silver-flecked sea as the ripples formed, and a sheer black wall of night. Thus, the trip down the Clyde was underway, and the first vibrations of the powerful steam turbines were felt. To my amazement, standing next to me was the first Bowser operator from Brize Norton. He had been posted to #70 Maintenance Unit. He told me I had brought the luck of "A" Squadron with me, stating since I had left there were ten fatal accidents for my successors to clean up.

With the hammocks now swinging, the boys began to see the fun in each other trying to master the method of placing oneself within them, without turning completely upside down. I succeeded in staying put, after the fourth attempt. Then, I realized that my best friend throughout this trip was to be my life jacket, which I had left lying on a bag, far out of reach beneath me. A slight roll to my right soon placed me on the deck, on all fours. I quickly learned the act of kicking my feet over the side first, to remain upright on landing.

Around 5:00 a.m. on the following morning, it was evident that a very strong swell was running, and to those in hammocks came the sensation of remaining constant at the base of a pendulum swing. Upon opening my eyes to see the beams of the deck above pulling off some fine aerial work, I felt a queer sensation in the pit of my stomach. A trip to the fresh air was necessary, especially as the heat radiating through the steel structure made a terrible atmosphere below decks. So with a quick scramble into plenty of warm clothing, I grabbed up the life jacket (which must remain with you at all times), and with others, soon appeared on deck.

Dawn was breaking and the sea looked angry in shades of green with whitecaps everywhere. All around us, in many shapes and sizes, were scores of boats, including the battleship *Ramellies* to our port side, and another, the *Resolution*, toward the rear of the convoy. A number of smaller naval units, scattered throughout, were circumnavigating the convoy's perimeter. In all, some ninety ships were soon to be exposed, prey to lurking U-boats, that had the advantage of Eire being a neutral part of Ireland, with the use of Malin Head. The convoy was fast approaching this point, becoming more vulnerable to attack all the time. This was the case with all shipping from the Clyde, and those sailing to the North Atlantic from Liverpool and adjacent ports. Shortly, the lights became visible on our southern horizon, with the huge beam of Inishtrahull Lighthouse reaching far out towards us. It appeared that the convoy had slipped safely away from this bottleneck, although it was reported that two U-boats had been sunk earlier that morning.

The first call for breakfast rang out, so our small group decided to shave and clean up before we received the second call, twenty-five minutes later. On arrival at the ablutions, we discovered to our horror that the fresh water was turned off until noon. Owing to the vast number aboard, this was to be a commodity in very short supply.

At ten in the morning, boat station signals sounded throughout the entire ship, and without exception everyone on board had to muster at their given boat station. This was to be a daily routine for the duration of the voyage. Already, the sea was showing signs of rough weather, making land-lovers legs most unstable, but boat drill is a necessity at sea regardless of conditions and the elements. Roll call was taken, and a group captain, possibly of the 266 Fighter Wing, inspected the personnel as though they were standing guard at Buckingham Palace. His complaint referred to "unshaven personnel on parade," paying no heed to the fact of the scarcity of fresh water in the steerage quarters. He stated, with emphasis, "Salt water soap is available in the canteen!" It did chafe, irritate, and leave the face sore. It was impossible for me to use. I saved tea from breakfast, and overcame what might have been a big problem. The most sought-after answer to the question, "Did this rationing cause the inconvenience of all aboard?" was never given.

By supper call that first day, it was evident that many had fallen to seasickness, but the meals served were extremely good and inviting, so those who could make it to the dining room did exceedingly well for themselves. I soon discovered that the more one ate, the more settled was the tummy. Also, I could not go along with the saying, "Stand at the gunwale and look at the horizon, and you will not become nauseated" because this horizon was erratic.

As the swell increased, the ship began to tell its age. The straining metal moved and groaned as we dipped and rolled along. We soon realized there would be a constant volume of noise as long as we were moving; adding to this, each time the rudder was put into play, the connecting mechanism would clang. With the motion rocking the hammocks, everybody was soon asleep, and as the night progressed, so did the turbulence and noise.

My pal, Tich, and I were quite surprised to find ourselves still going strong when the gale finally hit on the morning of the third day. The force of the storm had reached unknown proportions as the ships forged along very slowly to the speed of the slowest boat (nine knots). Navigation was very difficult with so many ships which must maintain code zigzag patterns to counter possible U-boat attacks. We stepped out onto the promenade deck, and faced a wall of water as the ship made its descent into the trough. This compelled us to cling onto the rails to prevent us slipping down the deck as the water gradually fell back and leveled out. At the same time, the bow was lifted upwards until we were set high on the crest of a wave. It revealed a magnificent view of the convoy, covering several square miles, being pitched and tossed mercilessly. White-capped waves, of startling green, churned to foam and swirled in all directions.

As we watched, there were boats taking the plunge, the bows dipped steeply, lifting their propellers, turning helplessly out of the water, with loss of steering and propulsion capabilities. One of these was a small freighter of the Blue Funnel Line. Each time she took the plunge, her deck cargo began to shift toward the gunwale. Those on the deck of the *Empress* witnessed one of the seafarers' worst fears, and watched helplessly as the freighter crew struggled to dump the cargo overboard. This was a tremendous task, because it consisted of heavy, transport vehicles facing the wrong way, and these had to be turned so they could run over the side when the boat listed.

The *Empress* was experiencing the same crescendos. As the stern of the boat left the water, there was a sudden increase in the velocity of the props. This caused a tremendous vibration throughout the boat, and as the prop re-entered the water with a crashing bang, it created a sudden shudder, shaking its guts as the velocity was reduced.

The squadron answered roll call on the port stern deck. From this point, we could see the *Ramillies*. She appeared to be battened down; with her fifteen-inch guns beneath the horizontal position, and full ballast, she ploughed straight through the waves as though totally submerged. It was on the fifth night of sailing that a tragedy hit the boat. Two gunners of the army personnel were killed while negotiating the raised doorsill in the steel deck bulkhead. They had just been relieved of their watch at the six-inch gun on the aft deck, when the force of the gale slammed the heavy steel door into them. That evening, very few people were in the dining room, but Tich and I still made the grade, and ate sumptuously.

This condition lasted without respite for six days, and throughout this time, a severe problem of drainage in the steerage washrooms occurred due to the disruption of normal run off. It was not unusual to paddle to the heads. Auxiliary facilities were installed at the stern end of the prom deck.

It was not until the ninth day at sea, with our position west of Greenland that the gale finally subsided. The convoy's speed picked up and headed for the eastern waters of Canada. After the war, the captain of the *Ramillies* stated, "It was the worst storm ever to be recorded in the North Atlantic, with waves attaining the height of ninety feet." I can vouch that it was a tremendous wall of water, reaching a great height as the ship lay low in the trough. When on the crest of a wave, one seemed air borne.

One advantage to the convoy was that the gale gave protection from the German submarines. Thus, it was possible to sail unharmed, through the Atlantic "no man's land," and the most vulnerable point of attack. The expanse of the Atlantic was just too wide for complete air support from east to west.

# 8

—

## *At Sea & a Changed Destination, "Java"*

At muster stations on the tenth day, the group captain made another visit to 242 Squadron and made further remarks about our complexions. At least the boys had tried to shave, to the extent of buying salt-water soap. What a painful operation! He was a group captain who, I thought, had not enough experience to be at the helm of a mobile squadron, or to understand its functioning as a battle unit. Regardless of rank, men work and fight together to keep plane and pilot in the air, as long as they need to be on the job. These boys had worked as many as twenty hours a day for up to six weeks, during the Battle of Britain. They came out clean-shaven and smarter in appearance than those who were still square bashing, and who had yet to face the enemy and soil their pants in fright. It was unity and co-ordination among officers and the ranks that made the better fighting units. This group captain did not earn any respect from these ardent fighters.

As the convoy headed south, the sea became quite calm, with schools of flying fish or porpoises suddenly appearing between the lines of boats. Visibility was extremely good now, which enabled me to stroll slowly around the ship and view the rest of the convoy all about us. It was a magnificent sight, so peaceful, with a faint swishing sound as the powerful ship's bow sliced the water to the rhythmic hum of the turbine engines.

Apart from the possible meeting of an armed surface raider, this huge muscle of power had reached intact, a point that was momentarily free of war. This enabled the men to relax on the decks in the warm breezes, playing bridge, chess, bingo, or reading the many books made available by swapping among each other; or merely to sleep and bask, permitting our bodies to absorb the sun, being cautious not to burn.

For twenty-four hours a day, vigilance was maintained at all vital points throughout each ship, especially the watertight doors. These would be slammed home tight in the event of an attack. Once these doors are all secured, the ship's interior is like that of a honeycomb, adding many times the chances of staying afloat if hit in several places during an attack. Every man served his turn on such fatigues during the trip, which was lonely and monotonous. Reading was not permitted, as the chances of falling asleep would increase. Many men found it very difficult to remain awake, owing to the intense heat throughout the ship, although every available air conditioning fan worked steadily throughout the day and night.

The skies had been quite clear for days, but this morning the cloudbank ahead toward the east gave an indication of land being quite close. This was true; Gibraltar was approximately one half-hour sailing before it would be visible over the horizon. Suddenly, the whole convoy made a ninety-degree turn, and we were sailing south again. Naturally, this caused some consternation among those on board, and foremost in our minds, where to now? A few days later several of the transports, including the *Empress of Australia,* dropped anchors off Freetown, a port of Sierra Leone, West Africa. Within the hour of arrival, a tender came alongside, bringing two native engineers. They came aboard clad only in "G" strings; their ebony bodies shone in the intense heat of the sun. Their task, of unknown magnitude was deep down in the engine room, where a fractured bearing on one of the main propeller shafts had to be replaced.

It was evident that the enemy had received some success here, for there were two freighters sunk on the northern reaches of the river, sitting on a sand bar with their super- structure visible and well above water. It was now considered quite safe, so the blackout restrictions were lifted. Entertainment was planned for deck performances under the stars, in the cool of the evening. In all, five glorious nights were spent here. The ship's crew built a stage over the swimming pool on the aft deck, with the electricians doing an excellent job with foot lights, and varied spot lights from higher points surrounding the pool. The most amazing thing, to everyone's pleasure, was the tremendous wealth of talent on board the *Empress.* They presented everything, from the old music hall through to grand opera, with some marvelous performances from talented instrumentalists. This was a Godsend to many, as it took ones' thoughts away from worrying about what had been left many miles away, and the possibilities that were lying ahead.

The days were unbearable from the heat and lack of breeze. Beneath decks, it was difficult to breathe, let alone eat. Because of this, it was requested of command that Christmas dinner, 1941, be served in the evening, to enable the boys to enjoy the spirit of the season, with the excellent menu of the ship's chief chef. Regretfully, this was refused, and tons of delicious food passed through the scuppers for the lack of appetites.

During those days at anchor, the natives would visit alongside the ship in their canoes, some bringing with them small articles to sell as souvenirs. Others brought fruit, and the occasional one came to give a display of diving. Of course, one paid for such a spectacle, but was also well rewarded by the feats performed. The water was extremely clear, and the human eye (unaided) could penetrate it for a great depth; this permitted full coverage of a diver's descent.

The natives were ebony black in colour, but with white palms of their hands and soles of their feet. They were of fine physical structure, the skin reflecting iridescent shades of blues, browns and reds in the sunlight; an attractive and handsome looking race, with tight, jet-black, wavy hair, the envy of any lady seeking that illusive permanent. A spectator would take a silver coin from his pocket and flip it overboard into the water. Immediately, three or four others followed suit, and in short order, several coins were suddenly entering the water. The divers, sitting quite erect, each in his individual canoe, watched those coins falling adjacent to him.

At first, it appeared that the diver was unconcerned about those little pieces of silver showering down; the first pieces to fall had now attained quite a depth. Then, with a little kick into the air, he turned and entered the water head first, barely making a ripple as he swiftly moved down, by-passing the silver. Retrieving the deepest pieces first, he rolled onto his back and plucked up each piece as it descended down upon him. Slowly rising, he surfaced, and like a tiddly-wink, he was sitting back in the canoe, waiting for further temptations to seize. The control of his breathing was exceptional as at no time did he show signs of fatigue.

After the third day, this sport was proving to be quite costly, so some of the boys reverted to deceptive methods by using the tin foil wrapping from chocolate bars. This would be neatly wrapped around copper coins (usually pennies) which gave the appearance of large pieces of silver, like a half-crown. Naturally, the divers, seeing such wealth approaching them, dived and swam vigorously, until they had detected the visitors' ruse, then all hell broke loose from this fine body of men, using profane language and cursing those responsible in terms they did not understand.

They were merely repeating phrases, like parrots, which they had heard from other visiting sailors of days gone by. Such happenings as these, small as they may appear on the surface, are the very things that have multiplied in the various new native countries, and created so much mistrust of each other today. The white man has not only exploited and ravaged these people to suit his own ends, but has degraded himself so much that these new countries, through united strength, will virtually crush him if goodwill, faith, and the acceptance of these people as equals (plus giving them the necessary support and assistance) is not soon accomplished.

After five nights, we were sailing again, with numerous schools of flying fish breaking the water's surface. At night, the constellation of the Southern Cross illuminated the sky with countless millions of stars, which form the Milky Way. The boys were enjoying the afternoon's games-practice in readiness for a deck sports day, to be held a few days later, when, on the horizon, a huge, black mass of clouds appeared and approached the convoy quite rapidly. To most, this was an unfamiliar sight. The massive form reached high into the sky, with no distinct shape; its edges, misty in appearance, melted away into the sunshine. Gradually, it enveloped the ship, drenching any person who failed to take shelter in time. This was a tropical storm lasting between ten and fifteen minutes, with tremendous force pouring out hundreds of gallons of water, and subsiding as quickly as it had started. It passed on into oblivion, to the north, leaving the ships once more in glorious sunshine.

Within minutes, the decks had steamed dry, with everyone back at his task as if nothing had happened. Sailing at night along the west coast of Africa, we were entertained by the many electric storms of terrific dimensions that were raining terror and devastation over the land. These storms were truly nature's fireworks at play, giving spectacular displays of patterned brilliance.

On such voyages, time or dates mean very little, but January 1, 1942, came, with Table Mountain rising above the horizon. Later that morning, a part of the convoy steamed majestically into the huge, natural harbour of Capetown, leaving sharks, whose dorsal fins were quite prominent above the surface of the water, playing at the entrance of the bay.

Capetown, and its surrounding countryside, small towns, beaches, people and their hospitality, is beyond description. Within one hour of docking, thousands of cars rolled onto the docks; the residents came to welcome the boys, take them home, and show them another part of God's universe. Here, Tich and I were the guests of an elderly lady who treated us like two lost sons, and offered so much if we would return and become a part of South Africa after the war. Her family welcomed us as if we were their own kin; questions were never asked. Africa entertained guests well, taking them on scenic drives and for a day at Muizenberg Beach (one of the worlds finest). We saw the views from atop Table Mountain, and motored through the orange groves. Large meals in the evenings were followed by a night at one of the finest theatres, then a return to the boat to sleep and await the car the following morning, to start out again.

To show that those at home were not forgotten, the boys shopped and shipped home thousands of hampers and gift parcels. This was made possible through the generosity of the residents, as service pay would never have covered on-shore pleasures too.

On the sixth morning of our stay, the residents who appeared were in far greater numbers than on previous days as they, too, knew it was goodbye. Soon, one by one, the big ships began to glide away from the dockside, and the many hawsers that had held them fast slipped into the water, and were drawn on board. The shouts of farewell and affection were heard among the many thousands standing on the quayside, and, as soon as the last ship was in line (astern to the others), the huge multitude of people burst out into song, "Auld Lang Syne," followed by "Will ye no come back again." Many a secret teardrop fell that morning, swelling the tide, from both gunwale and quay.

And so for the third time, these units continued toward their unknown destination. The trip around the Cape of Good Hope was uneventful, except for two sperm whales blowing waterspouts, which loomed up on the starboard side in the early evening of the second day out. The ships that by-passed Capetown were entertained at Durban, East Africa, in a similar manner. They sailed in time to meet the other ships and all boats came under strict blackout restrictions, due to the uncertainty of possible hostile units in and around Madagascar. If one recalls the fall of France, there were a number of French naval boats that did not follow their government orders to sail and join other Allied Forces. Instead, it was thought that they went to the French colony of East Africa.

# 9

—

## *Tropical Exploits*

The Japanese were now in the war. They had bombed Hawaii, Singapore, and taken Hong Kong. At this time, they were advancing south. The British battleships, *Prince of Wales* and *Repulse,* had been sunk by carrier-based planes from an attacking force of unknown dimensions. The warships had entered an engagement without air support, against an underestimated enemy. The odds against them were terrific, which was proven later.

These facts, and the convoy steaming north toward Aden, gave rise to speculation about entering the Mediterranean from the east, or swinging east to India, Ceylon, Burma, Singapore, Malaya, or the Dutch East Indies. However, a few days later, at a point close to Mombassa, the *Ramillies* and a few other boats left the convoy. We were now plying the waters of the Indian Ocean, placid and remote, yielding nothing but torridness. This unbearable, monotonous situation brought hardship to bear upon the men, draining them of much energy and causing mental fatigue. They lay around to conserve strength and absorb what little air came their way.

Relief came to the *Empress* when she broke convoy and entered the Maldive Islands, a small group some four hundred and seventy-five miles west of Ceylon. I claim that for beauty and colour, and to see Mother Nature at work, both in the water and on the surrounding coral, you could not travel anywhere more satisfying than in the Maldives. Our stay was for some four to five hours, in which time we were able to recuperate in the cool breezes floating past us from offshore. The pine trees, all standing at the same height as though sheared off, added their fragrance. The only thing standing taller was the flag-mast, with the Union Jack whipping at its head. This certainly was a most unusual sight.

An oil tanker of fair size came alongside and discharged its load into the *Empress.* The native crew was dressed in silk shirts and shorts of vivid yellows and blues, reds and greens, which added tremendously to the drab hull and dark, polished woodwork. With their job completed and the *Empress* refueled, we again started on our way to catch up with the convoy, now far ahead. Thus, a rendezvous with tropical splendour was over. With a burst of good speed, much-needed air was forced through the chutes to the lower decks where the boys settled down for a good night's sleep.

Upon taking her place once again in the convoy, it was obvious that certain boats had left and others had joined to continue the trek eastward. One of those leaving was the battleship *Resolution,* destined for a point to the north, either Ceylon or India. Among those who joined was the *H.M.S. Exeter,* after her survival and repairs from the Battle of the River Platte, and the old, notorious sister ship to the *Empress of Australia*, the *Empress of Asia*. This was a detriment to any convoy because of her coal-burning furnaces; it was difficult to control the heavy, belching smoke that would give away our position to the undetected enemy on the other side of the horizon.

In unbearable heat, the convoy ploughed on, ever eastward, to whittle down the next port of call to either Singapore, at the tip of Malaysia, or Batavia (now called Djakarta), on the island of Java. Suddenly, out of a very quiet afternoon, there was much hustling and nervous activity as the men of the *Empress* started to mount stairs, race through corridors, and across decks toward the port side of the ship. One man had shrieked out in panic, "Look at those poor bastards off to Singapore." At first, many thought this young fellow had become delirious from the heat, only to feel their own stomachs twitching as they gazed northward to watch a large portion of the convoy breaking away from us.

To me, this did not seem quite the right thing to do. Every ship had been a part of each other, heading towards a mission that should be accomplished together. This mighty muscle of power could flex its biceps as a tremendous force of displeasure to any part of the enemy that encountered it, but now it was divided, and naturally weaker. The situation was quite clear to me. An army of some twenty thousand personnel, fully equipped and equal to any Panzer division of the German army, was to be placed on a little, dry island, fully exposed to lethal attacks from the air. I call it a "dry" island because its reservoir was on the southern tip of Malaya, and the water had to be piped across the causeway to supply Singapore.

The 266 Fighter Wing, the only defence against air attack, sailed contentedly on into Batavia where we were far out of reach to defend these men. They never became established as a fighting unit, to prove their sting. On the afternoon of February 3, 1942, the *Exeter* dropped anchor in Batavia Bay, while the *Empress* was tugged into a berth of the modern Batavia docks.

Here, defeat was already showing itself. A boat that had been scuttled was lying upside down along the opposite side of the quay. Looking inland, one could see the beautiful greens and blues, which indicated the wealth of fertile soil. Seeing such a beautiful view, speculation grew that we might visit yet another garden of tropical splendour. It produced much needed banana and coconut palm groves, bamboo and passion fruits, fields of sweet potatoes, and rice paddies. Just after darkness had set, the old familiar sound of wailing sirens was heard. This passed without incident, and the boys realized that the task of equipping the Hurricanes for battle was just around the corner.

Personnel of 242 Squadron moved from the ship early on the fourth day of February. As we rolled away on the dock beneath the majestic bow of the *Empress of Australia*, our home for nine weeks, we felt that a good friend was now lost to us. We moved onto a fine highway, which led into a bright, modern city, exceedingly well laid out. There were extremely wide streets, treed boulevards, and a fine electric train transit system, fenced in on both sides.

It appeared that the Dutch were excellent settlers; the civic buildings, schools, and business offices were of the finest architectural design. Engineering feats were evident, especially bridges in the mountain terrain, the docks, and power stations. Commerce was thriving; all business being operated by the Javanese themselves. I learned later that the Dutch handled all government business, such as imports and exports, to maintain a balanced economy. There were many attractive residences, revealing the high standards in which many were living. The usual percentage of humble dwellers was most noticeable, especially in areas adjacent to the river.

King Wilhelm III School became base camp for the squadron. This was a building with palatial columns enhancing the whole of its frontage, a forecourt, and wide entry-steps slowly rising in white marble. It had a U-shape floor plan, and small classrooms with high ceilings and spacious windows, connected by shuttered verandahs circumnavigating the inner court of grass. There were no gymnasium, auditorium, kitchen, or showers, and very few toilets. Furniture did not exist, although there were some beautiful wall cabinets adorned with fine pieces of natural art by the students; included here were writing, charcoal etchings, water and oil reproductions, linocuts, wood etchings, carvings, and needlework.

The boys were happy when a truckload of mattresses arrived, as the thought of a marble floor for a bed was not comforting. Iron rations were the order of the day, owing to the limitations imposed upon the cooks. They were, however, lucky in obtaining a field urn for making a pot of tea. A pamphlet was issued giving a list of prices for various goods one might need to buy, also fares for rickshaws, pedal cars, taxis and trains. Here, the boys discovered their money stretched considerably farther, and a tendency to tip lavishly caused inflation for the civilian, which in turn created poor civilian relations and dissention towards us.

*Hollandia House* became the Allied Forces Centre, where the boys could eat well, enjoy a game of chess, cards, darts, or billiards. Until the various cargoes reached their destinations, one made good use of the facilities to be found here.

Aircraft Maintenance Group was now called upon to assemble and move the planes for action. The squadron personnel, ground defence corps, and flight workers were dispatched ahead to Palembang, an oil town in the centre of Sumatra, surrounded by virgin forest. Three or four days later, I found myself heading towards the northern part of Java in a train whose coaches were like cattle trucks, containing hard, wooden, bench-type seats. The wood burning engine belched out huge columns of black, sooty smoke, full of large pieces of red-hot cinders. It was impossible for us to open the window for fear of getting such particles in one's eye, even though the coach was far too hot and stuffy.

This was a journey of boredom, as the surveyor had chosen this route for the sake of joining points A and B, with little if any consideration for the pleasure of those who were to come after him. As for scenery, there was none, simply mile after mile of trees, a bridged creek or small river, then more trees. The vibration made reading impossible; gradually one was rocked to sleep. Then, with a little jump, your eyes would open with the mind saying, "Don't sleep, you are travelling in a strange country. You may miss something!"

Since my curiosity always got the better of me, I did manage to stay conscious enough to take in all those miles of trees. When we saw the ferry, it was immediately understood that a fair stretch of water was to be crossed before setting foot on Sumatra. This part of the journey was accomplished in beautiful sunlight, giving us magnificent views of some of the twenty thousand small islands that make up the great archipelago of the Dutch East Indies. Many years later, when I traveled through the San Juan Islands here in British Columbia, it brought back vivid memories of that far-distant waterway.

In this part of the world, there is little or no twilight; consequently, at 5:55 p.m. it is daylight, with total darkness arriving five minutes later. This happened soon after boarding another train, giving one the feeling of having entered into a trance, because the blackness outside had suddenly come to life with millions of little lights, dancing before our eyes. For the first time, I was witnessing fireflies in flight; the movement of their wings reveals the luminous part of the underside of the wing.

It seemed as though we had traveled many hours before coming to a halt at a lonely station in the jungle. Our small party, with two or three others, took leave of the train and bedded down for the remaining part of the night in a small warehouse standing nearby. To our amazement, we found it equipped with low cots, furnished with spring mattresses. So without further delay, I stacked my equipment alongside one of these and crashed, fully clothed, into a deep, deep sleep.

For some unknown reason, we stayed here three days; possibly for acclimatization, as this part of the world was very hot. What a wonderful sight greeted us on the following morning! We had alighted at a well-planned rubber plantation. In fact, we had stepped into some beautiful illustration found in a child's book of fairy tales. For myself, I found this place most intriguing. I recalled those social studies on world geography in my early days, and the wonderful description given by Miss Greene, who had traveled extensively throughout the Far East.

We took the liberty to accompany the tree tappers, watching them expertly wielding their sharp machetes as they channeled the bark, down which the sticky sap would flow. This white, milky solution would spill out of the vertical incision into a small cup attached at the channel base. Another group of men (like all the natives in these parts, naked save for a pair of coloured shorts) carried containers to collect from the cups as they filled. These collections varied in quantity from tree to tree, partly due to the amount of time that had elapsed from the day it was first tapped. This fluid would be transferred into large, round, flat pans approximately eighteen inches in height by six feet in diameter, where it would start to congeal. After a few days, this process seemed to be hastened by using a mechanism that was like a modern-day cake mixer. Gradually, the solution became stiff, whereby it was then baled up into cube-shaped packets wrapped in palm leaves. Later, it would be trucked away for further processing in some factory, possibly situated half way around the world.

Native foods had become quite a large proportion of the daily meals, and in most cases, it was found quite palatable and interesting. The various side dishes to the rice course and the tropical fruits, we ate with some caution. We had so often been warned as to the possibilities of what one could contract from such food, especially that which had to be handled by the local people themselves.

We continued northward on a long train journey, arriving at the large station of Palembang, Sumatra. It was situated on the southern side of a huge river (the Musi), with the city on the north side. Here, we met up with the rest of the boys, and learned that the aerodrome, Palembang #1, was north of the town and river. Transportation was very slow, being by barge. This would cause problems for those of us in the stores section. If, and when supplies arrived, what should receive priority was one of the hardest things to determine. Therefore the supply business was not only in jeopardy, but left in abeyance until the first shipment arrived.

The billets we found in a school (obviously designed for day operations only) were elevated concrete and tile floors, with posts holding tiled roofs above them. This gave excellent protection from the elements, sun and rain, but the cold night air penetrated everything, as there were no walls. Of course, the usual allies, the mosquitoes, were in full force, flitting around the bright lights, waiting to seize upon any bared flesh as one undressed for bed. The odd one would get inside your mosquito net.

# 10

---

## *Sumatra Attacked*

A few of us made a trip the following evening, into the heart of Palembang. We crossed the river in a large sampan, skillfully oared by an expert seaman who made the trip in thirty-five minutes. These boats are exceedingly well constructed, with an appealing design following dynamic curves right through its length and breadth. They have a snug cabin, low, but comfortably furnished with heavy cushions of fine materials and brass ornamented fittings and lamps: warmth, combined with protection from strong swell, being the first consideration of the boatman. Once in town, we found it difficult to find our way around due to the blackout restrictions. However, a fine restaurant loomed up, so we spent lavishly on an excellent meal. Then, by rickshaw, we found a large cinema showing the film "Come Live With Me" (by luck, with subtitles), with Dorothy Lamour and James Stewart. Unknown at the time, this was to be our last touch with civilization and a movie for over three years.

At 9:00 a.m. on the morning of February 10, news arrived that a trainload of supplies was ready for unloading at the terminal. Our duties would be gaining momentum from now on. In the yard, we met groups from each of the other two squadrons and H.Q. section. As expected, the amount of goods was far from being adequate for all of us, so a sharing of essentials was imposed; this would be done at the aerodrome. One thing we did note, the yard was well stocked with ack-ack cannon shells (Beaufor 40 and 20 mm respectively), and they were too far away for use where they would be most effective.

It had just turned ten in the morning, and before unloading commenced, the first sounds of ack-ack were heard across the city. Looking north, we saw five planes flying south. This told of a start to hostilities. Doors were open and we were surprised to see paratroops, and not bombs, fall out of their bellies. Apparently, on the evening before this attack, an officers' meeting had taken place, and they were instructed that, if such attack came, a retreat to Java must be made. Such a statement could have caused the pandemonium that broke out at the aerodrome. Circumnavigating the perimeter were the ground forces of three squadrons. It was understood that the officers and others were in, or adjacent to, the watchtower, and the main gate was practically free of defence.

The Japanese made an effective drop in this area, and quickly had the main gate (the only entrance to the aerodrome) sealed off. Thus, the staff cars, now loaded with officers and officialdom, were sitting ducks as they tried to drive free from the onslaught that followed. The boys on the aerodrome sat tight, then gradually, under command of their sergeants, moved forward and by nightfall had disposed of approximately two hundred Japanese, the estimated number in the drop. Thus, first blood was in our favour, but all means of continuing were lost because those vital to operations were now lying in pools of blood, annihilated in their own cars.

We, at the railhead, were helpless in as much as the river divided us. The officers' statement, "fall back to Java", meant only one thing; we would have to travel in what we had, one old truck. Not one of us possessed anything other than what we were wearing and carrying: tropical shirt and shorts, socks, shoes and topi, rifle and ammo, water bottle, and gas respirator. Ahead of us lay the unknown depths of jungle, poor roads if any, with the possibilities of trekking without food and water. Therefore, into the old truck (which was our only means to transfer supplies) jumped twelve men, including one officer, to commence a two-day retreat to a port, Oosthaven, at the southern tip of Sumatra.

A few hundred yards down the road, we met our first obstacle; the gas station attendant refused to fill the tank. Without question, a revolver was drawn while a second man helped himself to our requirements. To alleviate any repercussions for our actions, sufficient guilders, to cover the cost, were thrust into his shirt pocket. The truck moved out as quickly as possible. As we pulled away, more explosions were heard. The horizon filled with black smoke, north of the town. The Dutch had blown up the oil installation.

A half-hour drive brought us into the open country, with the road passing between fields and straddled with large trees. To our right, a ditched Hurricane fighter-plane lay in the centre of a field. This remained a puzzle to us, as no fighters had been operational from Palembang #1, and we surmised that it had left Palembang #2, which was in the vicinity, fifty miles to the south. With every precaution being taken against snipers, a man was dispatched to reconnoiter the plane without approaching too closely, with the additional green light to give assistance to the pilot, if still there. Due to the presence of the plane and unknown activities of the Palembang #2 aerodrome that morning, an immediate change of plans was made. We would take the alternative route to the south in the hope that progress could be made without further delays.

Our driver did his best to keep the truck rolling along, but found areas of the poor road surface difficult to negotiate. In addition, this road was similar to a switchback, containing many sharp curves with steep inclines and descents. Sudden braking and acceleration resulted in rupturing the brake-fluid pump, leaving the truck to charge down the slopes out of control. Due to deceleration on one such incline, we came to rest on the top of a hill. With light fading, the officer called it a day, and detailed guard duties for the night.

We had come to rest on a deserted road in the middle of the jungle; foliage of all descriptions was about us, with the branches of the trees interlocking each other across the road. Noises of many imagined predatory animals (some possibly two-legged) were heard that night by the various groups, as they each took their turn of duty. The sudden breaking of a twig, then the piercing shriek of something just caught for meat, caused one to halt in his tracks, turn without noise, breath held, to wait and see who would make the first move, friendly or hostile. Numerous little lights flickered during all hours of darkness, most of these being fireflies, but there were others whose owners we shall never know.

Not one of the men could say that he spent the night without tension, before or after, the shift he had been allocated. The question in my mind (since we were sleeping in the truck) was, will my buddies outside give ample warning for us to be positioned to resist, if attacked? If not, what will be my own line of defence? So, in a mechanical way of thinking, I fell asleep. The silence within the truck was broken. Simultaneously, three men sat up, each spluttering, "What was that?" There were another couple of shh's for quiet, while yet another said, "Lie down, you silly buggers. Joe farted." Moments later, one or two were snoring.

At first light, the wheels are put into motion, and Paddy pushed on regardless for the coast. The road worsened, and soon we were helping a number of natives cut down saplings to place over a large area of the road, presumably washed out by rain. Sufficient was laid to enable us to cross and carry on. Eventually, we could see that some sort of civilization existed ahead, but once more, the old truck decided to quit. The gas tank was dry. In a clearing we saw a huge house, standing high on stilts, fully constructed of bamboo. As we approached, a small crowd gathered and led us to a large wide staircase. The main entrance opened into a spacious room, well furnished and carpeted. A man sat in a large bamboo chair with an elaborate canopy. He welcomed us and learnt of our plight; we considered him head of the tribe. We were entertained with fruit drinks and some kind of scones. After a lot of explaining, he finally realized we were in need of gasoline, and supplied a can containing ten litres (a little over two gallons).

After many handshakes and thank-you's, we carried the can to the truck and continued on our way. In this type of terrain, the gas did not take us too far, but we did reach some pavement before stopping again. To our good fortune, the only traffic we encountered on this journey appeared. An old farmer with his cart drawn by a water buffalo towed us approximately a mile to a small native village and a garage. To our amazement, the mechanic was able to renew the broken pump—out in the middle of the jungle we purchased a Chevrolet spare part and a full tank of gas.

During the time taken to repair the vehicle, two of us scouted out a well-stocked grocery store. The bulk of the stock on the shelves was canned goods of both Australian and American origin. The man behind the counter was most business-like; his attire was complete with white apron and black bow tie. His failing was his inability to speak English. However, this was soon overcome with the appearance of the proprietor's wife, who expressed herself perfectly in the King's English. "It is of great pleasure to us both to have you fine gentlemen visit with us today."

We purchased our requirements and took our leave, receiving a beautiful smile that revealed a full mouth of gold teeth. Later, we discovered that the undertaker furnishes a funeral in relation to the value of gold he can extract from the mouth of the deceased person. I imagined she would receive the full treatment. I can recall my grandmother's statement of many years ago, "With an English tongue in your head, you may go anywhere, if you use it, and never will you be lost". This meeting with the grocer proved a point; she was not exaggerating!

The road maintained its twists and curves, its ups and downs, in and out of the deep shadows cast by the trees, which consistently lay across its path. This caused us to stay forever on the alert against any danger that might lurk around us. The Japanese' ability to jump ahead made us extremely cautious. On the evening of the second day, we entered the RAF Headquarters in the coastal town of Oosthaven. We were conducted to billets for a well-earned rest and received information of an early-morning boat leaving for Java.

The approaches to the docks were plugged with abandoned vehicles, making it impossible to park. Our officer directed Paddy alongside a row of these and shouted, "You're on your own; make the boat". We all baled out and dashed onto the pier to see the boat heaving its towlines, with the adjutant shouting, "Any more 242 Squadron, this way!"

I recall three of us tumbling over the guardrail, holding the balance of our grocery purchase. On board, we met (for the first time) three Gurkas from an Indian regiment. They had not eaten for many hours, so we shared our food with them during the trip across the Sunda Strait between Sumatra and Java. For most of this trip, we had torrential rains, which gave us excellent protection from enemy aircraft. The decks were covered with women and children who were unable to obtain a place on the liner that had left for Australia earlier that morning. Two days later, this liner was reported sunk by Japanese naval action, with no survivors.

# 11

---

## *Shortfall of Equipment, Catastrophic Losses*

We arrived safely back in Batavia (Djakarta), Java. Almost a week elapsed before all personnel of 242 were accounted for. Some had left Palembang #1 from the northwest side, which compelled them to follow tracks down the west side of Sumatra, through heavy jungle, before reaching a coast road that led them into the only port of exodus. A number did not fare too well, and upon arrival were hospitalized with malaria. Before their departure from the aerodrome, these boys had left their sting by cutting down the enemy, temporarily halting the Japanese advance. If the men within the tower that morning of the Japanese descent had disciplined themselves, distinction could have been theirs. Instead, it is a story of disaster that must be told. February 17 brought the end of hostilities in Sumatra.

Now, we were a squadron complete in personnel, but lacking the essentials to build a defence necessary to maintain the high standards of effectiveness expected of us. It was understood that fifty Hurricanes were shipped with the convoy, and at this point we needed them desperately, but where were they? Before heading north to Palembang, our maintenance division had been working on the assembly of these fighters, but we had not seen any for operational purposes. There was some speculation among the fellows that being fortunate enough to have remained a complete squadron, we would be on our way to another section of the front. (Hopes of landing in Australia or Burma were remote.) This was true, to the extent that we worked as a complete unit on the northern approaches to Batavia, Java (when the Dutch government declared all cities open), to keep them free of attack from enemy aircraft. As of February 18, the main target of the advancing Japanese army was Java, and its capital, so the squadron was compelled to leave our base camp at King Wilhelm III School.

Prior to changing our base, the personnel were still able to visit the city and service centers. This was laid out so attractively that one enjoyed touring it. Some of the boys wanted to visit those areas catering to their physical, personal instincts, which created a sudden influx of rickshaws and like conveyances for their use. The native driver took it to heart that time had caught up with the men, and that some means of transportation was required so that the desire for female companionship could be fulfilled.

One of the boys paid special tribute to one of the houses by stating that he had visited and had chosen a very attractive lady, who had taken him to her room to accommodate him. It soon became very evident that this was an impossibility when she screamed and vanished from the room. However, all was not lost by any means, for a few minutes later another lady arrived to take her place. The men had their pleasures and told about their escapades, but at short arm inspections that followed evening passes, the medical officer found some cases of venereal disease.

One evening in town, I encountered two sailors in Hollandia House, who had reached Batavia by unknown means. These two had survived, in some miraculous way, the sinking of *H.M.S. Prince of Wales.* During our conversation, I learned that one of them had actually been working with the ship's radar unit. He was convinced that his captain had gone all out to make himself the second Nelson, because he had completely ignored a thirty-six ship Japanese convoy of supply and troopships (unescorted), sailing on his starboard flank. The ships (approximately twelve in all) of the Allied Forces sailed right into the jaws of death, and put themselves at the mercy of far superior, and underestimated, forces of the Japanese fleet.

No RAF cover was available at that time, except for a few old, obsolete biplane bombers known as the *Wapiti*, that were stationed at the so-called, "Impregnable British Base of Singapore." These planes, under the gallant leadership of their squadron leader, did their utmost to press home an attack against such a formidable force, with little or no success. All planes were lost. The squadron leader took his own plane right into a Japanese battleship, but had failed to first switch on and fuse the bombs. This was the only hit scored from aerial retaliation. However, the *Prince of Wales*, with the aid of radar, displayed great courage and downed some seventy planes before she succumbed to countless odds. *H.M.S. Repulse* was also lost in this operation, before the smaller units withdrew. It has since been revealed that only two small boats accompanied the capital ships on this mission, and like the other units, they withdrew because of fuel shortage, and limped safely back to Singapore.

It was later said that signals were received from forward positions of the land units, that a landing of Japanese troops was taking place on the Malaysian coast, south of Kuantan. Allied naval units were heading into Singapore because of fuel shortages. Because of this alert, the *Prince of Wales* and *Repulse,* with two escorts, turned northeast to intercept the landing. However, they found it was only a herd of water buffalo on the beach which had created panic among the army defenders. I never heard whether or not this story was a hoax, and if because of it, the navy units were drawn into a trap. The Japanese were warned by native saboteurs, which led to the attack. At this point, there was no air defence over Singapore, Malaysia, or the straits. If Britain and her Allies were to prove they still had a sting, it must come from the balance of the fleet in co-operation with the boys of 242 Squadron, if aircraft were ever received.

"242, Attention 242—we are moving, possibly to Australia. Pack and be ready within the hour." This order passed rapidly between us one morning after four days of speculation about what we would be doing in the near future. Shortly after this, the trucks were assembled and loaded, in record time. The expectation of seeing the land of the Southern Cross, Australia, was overwhelming. The convoy moved off, with everybody in high spirits, toward the northern part of the city. Close to the city-limits stood the deserted Dutch army barracks. We turned into these instead of taking the road leading to the docks. Here, we learned that our role in this part of the globe was about to begin, and the aerodrome at Chillilitan, a few miles further north, would be the base of our operations. The cancellation of all passes (effective immediately) meant only one thing—work and sleep.

We were not located in the main buildings, but were confined to the wooden section at the far end of the courtyard, the interior of which resembled mule stables. Fortunately, we received mattresses, which kept us elevated from the concrete floor. Food was meager and scarce. We could buy some from the natives, but we were limited to fresh, whole fruit only.

This was considered a necessary precaution against disease, provided nobody was foolish enough to purchase items already peeled.

Reveille was at 3:30 a.m. The alarm clock was in the form of a dispatch rider's motorcycle, driven through the stables by a flight sergeant. After a splash of cold water to the face and a tooth brushing, we again took to the trucks and headed for the airstrip. Eighteen Hurricanes had been flown in from an aircraft carrier of the Indian Flotilla. They were equipped with twelve, Browning 303 machine guns. It was extremely hot, being only 6 degrees latitude south of the equator, and this created a major problem. The speed of the plane was drastically reduced by the heat, and the Rolls Merlin engines could only produce one hundred and eighty miles per hour, here, compared to three hundred and forty, over England. To compensate for this loss of speed, it was decided to arm only eight of the guns, reducing the effectiveness of a strike.

Immediately upon arrival, each section divided: half to work and half to breakfast. This was the day our Scottish cooks introduced me to porridge (oatmeal) served with salt; it was good! In this manner, the planes were ready by first light, and everyone had eaten, ready for any hostilities that might start.

The planes stood within compounds formed by huge piles of earth, in horseshoe shapes. Referred to as bays, they had camouflaged netting hanging from poles, to shield the Hurricanes from aerial view. We set up base in small huts, hidden in a densely wooded area north of the landing strip, where we were able to house the field cookhouse, medical services, armoury, and stores. From here, easy access was made to and from the planes, making maintenance and arming, quick and efficient.

Apart from the landing strip, the field had been completely shut off from use by the installation of poles, placed row upon row. These stood about six feet high, and were to thwart any attempts by hostile planes to land en mass, with units sufficient to take over the aerodrome. Additional natural barriers, the wooded area and a high bank dropping sharply to the paddy fields to our north, gave assistance to the defence units. Australian anti-aircraft units were stationed in the barracks to the west, and they controlled the perimeter from either end of our establishment.

Warning of hostile aircraft in the vicinity was given by striking large pieces of suspended bamboo with small sticks. This unusual sound became familiar to us throughout each succeeding day. Always, after our own planes had left on a westerly course, the Japanese Zeros approached and strafed from the east. Raids of this nature did nothing to us, other than being a nuisance and causing us to duck to miss a few bouncing bullets. An engine fitter, discussing a part with me away from the camouflage, received a bullet through his billowing shirt, which seared his back. As we ran for shelter, I was missed. We realized that while the Zeros were so deployed, our Hurricanes were able to cause some damaging setbacks to Japanese land units trying to cut in from the northeastern coastline, where they had landed.

One notable remark of the pilots told how the offensive was shaping up in our favour due to the stupidity of the Japanese soldier, who merely hid his face in the undergrowth, but left his rear-end exposed to the muzzles of eight machine guns. A push of the trigger poured out hundreds of bullets, causing thousands of casualties with abdominal wounds. As the pressure built up, so did the flight missions. On one day, seventeen such attacks were made. If the defending, Dutch-led, native army units had followed up, we would have won the first round for Java. However, on the following morning, we discovered that the army was behind us, with the anti-aircraft units about to abandon the aerodrome, and leave us as the front-line of defence.

To coincide with this sudden change of events, a change of tactics also took place. The Japanese were making the first bombing raid on our landing strip. The ack-ack gun standing immediately in front of me, packed and ready for the road, was suddenly swung into action, and promptly smashed the lead plane into oblivion. As this was the bombardier for the whole force of twenty-seven planes, and with a second plane bursting into flames a few seconds later, confusion prevailed among the remaining pilots. Finally, the bomb bays were opened and the bombs released, but too late to strike the landing strip. Instead, they hit the barracks, causing considerable damage and several casualties among the Australian soldiers as they prepared to leave. A third plane was struck out from the tail of the flight as it released its salvo of bombs.

With our planes still intact, and in view of the situation, it was decided to take 242 Squadron to a base behind the so-called, new established line. This meant a retreat to the southern side of the mountains, into a flying field adjacent to Bandung, effective as of the following morning.

The planes dispatched (sixteen sound, and one with aileron trouble), the convoy headed on its way towards the mountains. To our dismay, and only a few miles down the road, Dutch army officials confronted us and ordered us back; the roads were congested with hundreds of empty army trucks. Due to this turnabout, it would mean the picketing of the Hurricanes at Chillilitan for another two days, but greeting us upon our return were the usual twenty-seven bombers. This time, there was no ack-ack battery, so they sailed over, pouring another payload into the now empty barracks, leaving our units intact and unharmed on the southern perimeter of the aerodrome.

# 12

---

## *Capitulation*

The sun was already creating a low mist, indicating that a very hot day was forthcoming. As we climbed the mountain road, it gradually unveiled a scene of magnificent beauty. The base of the mountain was treed with manicured acres, like a flight of stairs. Some were flooded with water, and Javanese women were paddling as they planted rice plants. At a different level, men with water buffalo drawing a wooden plough were ploughing in the stubble from a harvested crop in preparation for replanting.

As a mobile unit, we used sixteen trucks of various sizes travelling several yards apart, with a water tanker following far behind. We were easy targets until we reached the timbered areas, far above the farms. A twisting road, with switchback sections and tree cover, was to our advantage, and provided little exposure to the bomber overhead, trying in vain to knock us out. At one point, the Japanese artillery entered the fray for a short distance, but the convoy plodded on. This is known and written of so often as a strategic withdrawal.

The descent led us through other farm areas producing sweet potatoes. Just before our entry into Bandung, a collision claimed the lives of two brothers. One truck lost its brakes and sideswiped the truck ahead of it. These were the first casualties for 242 Squadron. We arrived at the new zone by six p.m.

At this point, one could begin to take stock of the situation and the predicament of 242. It was obvious now that unity did not exist between the Dutch command and its native army units, or the air command. It was also apparent that fifth column activists had become successful in their operations, which included immediate attacks on the Hurricanes as they were picketed out on arrival at the new base. Here we suffered our first plane losses through the lack of protection and natural shelter. This move into Bandung merely exposed our strength showing just how few in numbers we really were. On the following morning, at 5:00 a.m. they hit hard again, with fighters strafing indiscriminately. The Zeros went about their business unmolested. Our maintenance crews were beaten to the punch and the surviving planes, still parked, were devastated. Later that morning, inspection proved our sting was finished. The Hurricanes had been reduced to two.

The Japanese claimed they were liberating Asia for the Asians, and gradually received native support as they advanced. The whole purpose of the Allies entering the Dutch East Indies was to defend the oil fields and to deter the Japanese attack long enough to enable British and American reinforcements to reach and strengthen the defences of Northern Australia. If our complete convoy had been diverted only to Java, instead of splitting us up, such a sacrifice would not have been made. The army still on board their ships was subjected to a savage air attack while trying to reinforce Singapore; all was lost. The air units in Sumatra, with their supplies stranded on the railroad, were in no position to give air cover. Little was left for the defence of Java.

Three of us were standing on the tarmac when General Archibald Wavell approached and welcomed us to Java. We felt beyond all doubt, that if he had received the full convoy intact, it would have reversed the outcome in the Pacific Campaign. Instead, he wished us well, shook our hands, and departed to India on February 25, 1942.

A number of B-17 Bombers (Flying Fortresses) were still standing, unharmed, on the opposite side of the field. This left us questioning why they had not been used along with our attacks on the enemy. Secondly, why were they not used to transfer 242 Squadron (which was intact and ready) to another front? Also, why weren't they destroyed? We later learned they were being held for Dutch Command, with government officials, to use on an escape bid to Australia leaving us to the care of the Allied naval units at some later date.

Several years later, after I had settled down in Canada, I discovered that the Japanese were able to use some of these Fortress bombers to great advantage when teaching their student pilots in tactical air attack. They could determine possible angles of approach with a lesser degree of danger to themselves. I read this account in a book written by a Japanese fighter-ace, which I purchased on the concourse of O'Hare Airport in Chicago, USA. The Fortress proved to be a formidable barrier to attacking fighter aircraft; they respected and held both the machine and its pilot in high regard.

On March 5, 1942, the 242 Squadron moved further south to an airbase near Tjilajap seaport, in anticipation of evacuation. From here, three Wapiti bombers left on Saturday night (March 7) hoping to reach Burma. I was told they failed to reach their objective.

Sunday, March 8, 1942, was a bright, sunny, peaceful day. It marked the commencement of a new era for Java. With its two Hurricanes as escort, 242 Squadron moved out into the mountains heading for the docks of Tjilajap and a rendezvous with the *H.M.S. Exeter,* and other units of the fleet. At a little past ten in the morning on this fateful day, the A.O.C. (Air Officer Commanding) drove up to meet us, in those beautiful mountains, with the news of the Dutch Capitulation. Following this announcement, he made the most astounding statement, which floored everyone. "British naval units had failed to make rendezvous."

Up in these clear, blue regions, we were directed into the tea plantation of Pamegatan, to take over the drying and processing plant for use as a temporary barracks. For the past thirty-three days, the squadron had done everything possible to organize itself as the fighting unit it had always boasted to be. One small unit was insufficient to cope with the situation at hand. The last communiqué from the Dutch East Indies read, with words to this effect, "Units of the Royal Air Force have withdrawn to the mountains, to carry on as guerilla units."

All guns and ammunition were packed in grease and burlap, then buried deep between the rows of tea plants, with latrines placed on top. (They might still be intact.) To pass the time of day, men would form small parties and take the mountain paths leading up to a clearing of rich, green grass. Here, they would sit down and listen to the birds and a swift-flowing stream, which ran alongside.

On one such morning, I joined the group. When I used my left hand, to steady myself into a sitting position, a small snake bit it. It bled quite freely, and I paid no further attention, considering it well cleansed. However, around three the following morning, I realized the mistake of not going to the doctor, for I was in a high fever, with my arm immobilized. As soon as roll call was over at six in the morning, my friends sought out the doctor. He lost no time getting me down to the planter's house where his wife (a registered nurse) assisted in the boiling and cutting operation. The scar on the back of my index-finger joint today measures 3/16 inches in length. At the time, it felt as though the scalpel had traveled the width of my hand.

The most unusual things found about the plantation were huge, trumpet-snout beetles. They basked in the sun all day, one astride the other, on the limbs of small trees. Their bodies appeared encased with armour plates, resembling warriors from ancient days. For two weeks, we existed on the bulk rations I had loaded back in Batavia, supplemented occasionally with goat, obtained from the natives.

Word came that unless we descended to the village of Wanaraja, the Japanese would blast us out with artillery. So, gathering up my few personal belongings, I joined the rest in one of several trucks, with my arm still supported by a sling. Slowly, we went to the small market town; here we became POWs, and the Japanese housed us in the mule pens. Food was very short, so when possible, we would barter with the natives at the fence, trying to buy a banana or pineapple with the little money we may have raised by previously selling some small article. Sentimental as they could have been, these small items meant survival, which by now was foremost in each and everyone's thoughts.

Bridge and chess started to be the main pastime, with the odd game of poker or crib being played. When the rain fell, it was so heavy that we huddled up together under the center portion of the roof to keep warm. If one got wet, he would sit out in the sun to steam-dry, which took only a few minutes in the intense heat. By this time, most of us had run out of soap and toothpaste. Little water was available, so dirty clothing and odors became a part of us. Long hair and beard growth also presented problems. This unnatural growth became irritating, causing one to scratch, which led in some cases to skin infections and mental tension. Slowly, the boys of 242 Squadron took on the appearance of slum dwellers, known in this day and age by the elite name of "hippie."

Three weeks later, in the early part of the evening, a curfew was imposed on the camp. The Japanese told us that in the small hours of the following morning we would be called, to start our journey to a new camp. This occurred about 3:00 a.m., and after a little time to eat, we started out on what was to be the first seventeen miles. Fortunately, the roads were not too bad and we whistled as we moved along, "It's a Long Way to Tipperary," or "Pack Up Your Troubles in Your Old Kit Bag." We kept a steady step, and made reasonably good time to the railway station. The drivers, with escorts, took the trucks ahead to the new destination of Semplak, an aerodrome near the inland pleasure-resort of Buitenzorg. The rest of us were hustled into coaches where we found the blinds had been lowered and remained that way until the train had left the built-up areas. I think everyone was surprised to find that the mode of conveyance was not cattle trucks!

Naturally, we needed to sit after this walk; it also helped us to relax and doze, pondering on the possible events in store at the end of this run. We noted as we sped along that there was no evidence to show a war had been waged until the train came to a stop. Here, we all left the train, one coach at a time, and saw that the bridge was destroyed. We walked down through a large ravine to another train waiting up on the other side. Other than the overturned boat in the harbour of Batavia, the oil storage-tanks at Palembang and this bridge were the only items we saw destroyed; we attributed this to the Dutch demolition squads.

We peeked through the blinds as we passed through the sidings of Bandung, and received another jolt, which did nothing for our moral. We saw, with mixed emotions, a complete train of flat-deck railcars loaded with long, clean, bright-white spruce and pine crates. One side had been ripped off, revealing the contents within: American fighter planes (Kitty Hawks, awaiting assembly), that could have bolstered our numbers to an unknown advantage.

Eventually, the luxury of the transit system came to an end, compelling us to face the hottest part of the day on a dusty road, fully exposed to the sun without the hope of shade. Distance became immaterial, as we knew that there would be no food or water until we had accomplished this transfer. The hot roads played havoc with our feet. The guards were also feeling the strain as they were in full dress, which was far more cumbersome than the light tropical clothing worn by us. Many feet were being dragged along as we tried to adhere to the raucous tones of these little bastards, who were ploughing their rifle butts into the backs of stragglers. The sun was almost down, which meant we would have to hasten our pace, or be trapped in the dark. The guards made sure we did not arrive after the short dusk, and (for once) they counted without error.

# 13

---

## *Wing Commander Alexander*

A huge plantation house, complete with colonnades and a slave platform in the centre foreground, was to be our place of existence for the next few months. The large rooms were of brick and marble, the floors of large flagstones. It was onto these stones that we sagged, partially propped against the wall, waiting for an announcement that food would be forthcoming. It arrived within the hour, a dry, tack biscuit, with a camp sausage (Australian) and a piece of bread. While we sat there nibbling, a single file of large ants started down the wall from a hole close to the ceiling. As they proceeded across the floor toward us, they traversed the area adjacent to the doorway.

Consequently, when a person walked through, he inflicted casualties among them. Immediately, those not injured shouldered the dead or injured, and passed them one to the other, all the way back to the hole. A piece of biscuit, approximately 3/8 inch cube, was placed in front of the ants still on the floor. This, too, was lifted in its entirety straight up the wall and into the hole.

So that I would not be exposed to the ants' exodus, I moved into a bamboo house that was elevated on a three-foot concrete slab standing in the rear courtyard. Here, we had the company of a King Lizard, perched high in the rafters. We also enjoyed some fine entertainment from a prehistoric looking insect, a praying mantis. This little fellow stood proudly on his hind legs to a full height of nine inches. He was always willing to take someone on in a boxing duel, under the Marquis of Queensberry rules. Also, he was forever present when our much-needed food was being served, waiting for a handout. Some fellows would grudgingly hand over just one grain of rice, the tightened belt already indicating early signs of starvation.

Soon after breakfast, which consisted of a small helping of plain, hot, soggy rice, we were called out on parade. This was our first encounter with the Commandant of the camp who, prior to the war, had spent four years at the University of Manchester, England, in Engineering. This may have had some bearing on the fact that our complement only worked one day out of three. We had entered this compound in three units, so each unit worked on an alternate day. We hoped that this Japanese captain understood the habits and conditions under which the white man could best exist. Were we being optimistic?

This day was considered by many to be a day of reckoning. Ahead of our three groups, there stood a single group of commissioned ranks. One man was missing from the group, Wing Commander Alexander. He had been interrogated the evening before, and ordered to lead his men to work on the aerodrome this morning. The officer had refused to comply with the orders, at the same time referring to a copy of the Geneva Conventions which he carried. He stressed firmly that to work POWs on military targets was contrary to the regulations. He was placed under close arrest. The Commandant made it quite clear that the Japanese would use the Conventions, but only when it was beneficial to them.

With our own commander gone, we were instructed in Japanese drill. This was meant to instill a better understanding of their proletarian troops, while under the jurisdiction of such a primitive and barbaric person. So, to satisfy their desires, we went through the motions: left turn, right turn, at ease, attention, and the bow—a seventeen degree, forward list of the trunk, without elevating the eyes or face when bent forward.

The group of officers was dismissed and had encouragement, (at least for the time being) that they would not be worked. Senior, non-commissioned officers marched their respective groups to work under duress. It was evident that operations had been initiated from this aerodrome; two hangars were completely destroyed, and the airstrip was potted with many large craters. A third building, resembling a barn, stood at the far end of the field, its floor covered with medium-size bombs. Our orders were to proceed to collapse the remains of the two hangars, whose superstructures were entirely of wood built upon concrete walls about four feet high. The bombs were taken by truck and dumped into a swamp, adjacent to the Batavia docks. Each truck received a nominal load and moved off, escorted by a guard.

A hedge separated the airfield from a native home where a large family of girls was living. The bombs, one hundred pounds each, were heavy and difficult to manhandle. It was a hazardous job to lift them into the trucks with the constant fear of our strength giving out and dropping them. There were no block and tackle available to hoist them on board. It was time absorbing, and while we laboured, the guards took turns visiting the girls behind the hedge.

It was obvious that a few days would be used to transfer the bombs, delaying the renewal of the runway. The discarded lumber was piled and burnt; a few of the posts were retained for battering rams. With the superstructure gone, the breaking up of the concrete began. This created a lot of hard work and resulted in sweating bodies smeared with blood from torn hands, arms and chests. Bruises and abrasions were caused as the surfaces of the posts hit us when they vibrated and bounced violently against the concrete. With some two dozen men pushing, each time a post fell forward a few chips would fly off, with amazing force and rhythm. Occasionally, we might be rewarded with a piece the size of a soccer ball. It was depressing and tiring work, especially when we were unaccustomed to working in such heat.

One evening, we were called to an area adjacent to the camp. We formed a long line from a compound attached to the room where the Wing Commander was imprisoned, to a storage house. From the compound, slowly there came an endless stream of four-gallon cans containing high-octane gas, which were passed or dragged between each of us. As the cans progressed upward and along the line, it so happened that several of them became lighter, or empty, before they had reached their final place in the storeroom. The occasional dull thud of a dropped can meant the splitting of its seam and contents lost. The many cans dragged caused further losses through small punctures. Consequently, unless you kept an eye on the can, the fine, jet-spray of gas would stream over your legs and feet with a cold, spirit effect, such as with methyl hydrate. The only disadvantage to this persistent sabotage was the stench; the air reeked of gas.

The guards were furious upon sensing the losses and vented their anger; rifle butts crashed on ribs or boots, on shins or feet. We eventually had the transfer accomplished, much to the detriment of our Wing Commander.

Each man soon understood the importance of staying alert at all times. When a guard entered the room, the first fellow to spot him immediately shouted out, "joski," which called the rest of us to attention. All would bow in salute. If a guard was met while walking the grounds, you would stop and salute. Failure to comply resulted in corporal punishment, a jab with the rifle butt or a punched face. Some of the fellows were hung up by their thumbs for several hours as a warning to others.

# 14

---

## *A Hole of Infestation*

"All men must remove the hair from his head." This was a direct order from the Commandant. The camp barbers were put to work at once, supplied with old implements with poor edges. Many of us received sore scalps trying to get the hair shaved off as closely as possible. If a guard could hold a hair from any man's head between his fingernails, the punishment was a number of slaps on his face. So, we were bald on top but still had facial hair, displaying moustaches and beards in various combinations of shapes and sizes. This later led to a very good competition and something that was an impossible thing for the Japanese to accomplish. Sergeant Rich grew the finest full beard I have ever seen.

With the bombs gone and the gas removed, we were only left with the job of filling holes. Trucks were now deployed, with one guard and four POWs, to range out over the countryside in search of stones, a task that became increasingly difficult. The guard would not permit the truck to go off the highway. We could only scrape up small quantities of flint, which lay scattered under the hedgerows. This work involved only one group each day. Those remaining in the camp were free to attend a class of their choice, mathematics, shorthand, art, or to play bridge and chess, etc. There were also chores to do: washing clothes and bedding, housekeeping the area, and bathing, (showers without soap).

I used the opportunity to take Pitman shorthand classes, which enabled me in quite a short spell to write forty words per minute. The teacher, who was exceedingly good, hailed from the faculty of the Pitman College in London, England. He was an AC2, (aircraftman second class), the lowest rank of the R.A.F. Somehow, money and commissions go together. It was hard luck; he was the son of a Welsh miner, a brilliant man, and superb in English, but now just an AC2. It was under similar circumstances that the mathematics instructor, (a Canadian), who was a LAC, (leading aircraftman) from a London suburban secondary school, had remained a radio operator. Before enlistment, he had spent considerable time as a logger, in several camps along the British Columbia coast. His spare-time was devoted to astronomy.

I do not know if either man survived the war.

It had become customary in the evenings to watch or play soccer. Due to the heat, the match would be one-half hour each way, two matches per evening. Everybody enjoyed this break, including the Japanese. Competition was keen, each section fielding a team. Section C3, of which I was a part, did extremely well. An amazing amount of stamina was used, and many were surprised that we could remain so fit and strong considering the small, under-nourishing meals we received. Breakfast was rice or barley cooked in water, rather stodgy, with no milk or sugar. Lunch consisted of the same amount of rice, with three spring onions. Supper was rice, about the same amount again, with a little cabbage soup (so little cabbage, that we thought it was washed today, for use tomorrow). This daily menu existed unaltered for six months.

There was a large contingent of officers; several had arrived from other units that were in Malaysia. It was understood that money for a pay parade had been withdrawn, so we did not receive any pay. Dr. Dawson made a request for money, to acquire much-needed medical supplies. He was flatly refused, so he then withdrew from the Officers' Mess and made his quarters in the sick bay. What money he had was used to purchase liver, for a patient dying from anemia and for other items needed to maintain a sick bay, such as cotton batten, aspirins, and iodine. Because of bruises, scratches and abrasions, the sick bay was forever increasing its number of resident patients.

One morning, I also became a casualty, with two large, tropical ulcers opening up: one on the left thigh, and one on the right buttock. Ulcers eat into the flesh, expanding their circumferences as they progress deeper, cutting a cavity the shape of a basin. They cause a constant, nerve-throbbing pain. The Doctor's treatment was to feed it sufficient cod liver oil to try to arrest the penetration. If this was achieved, it might complete its life cycle and die within the immediate area of the basin. Periodic douches of permanganate of potash were used to wash and cleanse the area of all dead matter, but on every occasion, deeper potholes were found beneath the surface of the basin floor. Thus, Dr. Dawson (our Squadron leader) turned to his last resource. This was a May & Baker formula; the only prescription in his possession, and one he was reluctant to use. Always in his mind was the possibility of something more demanding that would require it. Nevertheless, because so much was achieved in two applications, (each retained for three days before removal), he was able to discharge me with good results. He went about the process of cleansing three others in the same manner. I had been constrained for nine weeks and had become fearful as to when I might have the pleasure of walking again.

During that time, we were visited on two separate occasions by high-ranking Japanese officers. The second one, who I thought was the General in Command of the southern forces, would have been delighted to see us all dead, rather than the mess he witnessed as he passed between the cots. I came out of that hole of infestation and mass of decaying human flesh to play another game of soccer within two weeks, and scored two goals. I went back to the aerodrome feeling a little weak at the knees, but determined to carry on.

The concrete walls were removed and the potholes all filled, except for one, a large crater that divided the airstrip into two parts. The truck driver, who had brought us through Sumatra, had been taken to Batavia where he was assigned to bring an old steamroller through the mountains to the aerodrome. This was a tremendous task for one man; the old, iron relic required endless quantities of water and fuel which meant constant stopping to cut wood or pump water.

Meanwhile, the problem of finding fill still existed; the crater required a lot of rock.

Unlike previous occasions, we suggested ripping the stone lining from the culvert which drained the field. Finally, the Japanese consented to the plan. With great gusto, and a spurt of unexpected energy, a group of us fell upon the stones, thereby wrecking a main section of a complex draining system. Gradually, the stones were dropped into the vast, abysmal opening, taking far more than was at first anticipated. Here, the old R.A.F. cliché, "Press on

regardless," gave momentum to a rapid tearing apart of a much-needed drain. In return, it was a warm and silent reward for us that so much havoc was accomplished by this act of "sanctioned" sabotage.

Four days had passed since the steamroller had left Batavia heading to its new job.

It chugged along through mountainous terrain, barely finding sufficient power to reach the summit of treacherous climbs, or the braking ability to negotiate precipitous curves on its descent. It plunged downward, with ever increasing momentum from its own weight. Amidst loud cheers and catcalls, it finally rolled out onto the airstrip, the boys waving it toward their quarry of stone.

With full throttle, the driver permitted the steamroller to race toward its objective, only to push its roller over the edge of the crater and sink to the axle. Silence fell immediately. The driver was hauled down from the roller and punched several times about the face. In a rage, the guards slapped the smirk off any other man whose lips showed the slightest curvature. The broken edge of the crater revealed that much more material was still required (just to help withdraw the steamroller, without considering the rest of the crater), before it could be rolled. Several more days passed before the machine was freed and the final rolling took place.

The work at the aerodrome was finished. A few days slipped by before a party was formed to cut grass around the Japanese quarters. The cuttings that resembled hay more than clippings, were left in piles at various points on the grounds. That same afternoon, the guards grabbed a bunch of us, to get these piles of grass removed. Two fellows stepped forward, bent over, and practically had one pile contained in their arms. From this pile came a loud hissing sound and a large, black python uncoiled. Three or four of the boys, brandishing tools, went to the aid of the two men. The big snake was left writhing on the ground, chopped into pieces; the estimated length was five to six feet.

Between the days on which we did chores, we amused ourselves. Several of the boys had become good chess players. Five leagues were formed to keep competition keen; the boys were occupied and free from trouble. Others were happy to learn the art of contract bridge and to overcome the difficulties in bidding. A few individualists set themselves tasks in their favourite hobby; there were some artists, wood whittlers, and model makers. During the six months at Semplak, the Japanese Commander had from time to time passed by various groups not detailed for work that day. He had seen very interesting objects or pictures taking shape, and to everyone's surprise called for a show to be staged. One sergeant had put all his interest into making a five-octave keyboard and this gave my friend, Reg, and me the inspiration to try to make an organ. I had started to shape the cone, for the base of a pipe, at the time the show was called.

A date was set to coincide with the completion of most items under way at that time. The Commandant made several requests of the creators that he be allowed to take their displays and keep them as souvenirs. One piece that caught everyone's eye was a whittled cabin cruiser made by a Canadian from Sooke, BC. Created with the finest of detail, it was a model of the boat this young fellow desired to build upon his return home. There were no refusals that day and the Commandant left with all he had requested. One of the guards was a schoolteacher from Tokyo and he spoke with a good command of English. He made a request of me, with two others to sing and teach him the words of the songs we whistled when marching. They were "Pack Up Your Troubles in Your Old Kit Bag," and "It's a Long Way to Tipperary." He was smart, and learnt the tunes quickly.

Tropical rains came and passed in huge masses, as though they were passing swarms of locusts. We had awaited these since our job on the airstrip had come to a close. Two plane transports and a number of Zero fighters had paid a couple of visits. There would be no more; our job had left the field a quagmire. We had completed the assignment at Semplak.

Native peddlers going to local markets, traversed the same road carrying all wares upon their backs, or in containers strung on long poles that hung heavily across their shoulders. In some cases, the weight would be terrific, buckling the knees of the carrier as he jogged to a mindful rhythm. These were invariably carrying live fish, but very little water was lost. On occasion, one of the peddlers would stop with the hope that some POWs, still having money, might buy the odd egg, banana or pineapple, or a can of milk, vegetables, or steak (of an unknown date) from American packing houses, or possibly stolen from some disbanded military base.

Then, there would be the sudden noises of light tinny music and very small bells, which told of a procession approaching. It would appear with a number of bearers carrying a light carriage, bedecked with an ornate canopy. The adorable bride and groom sat inside as they wound their way to a place of marriage, all dressed in their best and carrying small lighted candles.

Water buffalo were used to draw carts containing various articles of commerce. This was the only mode of conveyance available to tradesmen and the local people. They appeared to be an inoffensive animal, but were regarded by many to be quite vicious if roused.

# 15

---

## *Camp Makasura*

The day arrived when we were hauled out of bed and put on the march again. This would be an agonizing experience because we had all averaged a weight loss of sixty pounds. Many of the boys were in a very weak condition through malnutrition, and footwear had become a problem; distances took a toll on men and feet. Having already passed over the area to the station, we remembered certain landmarks and were able to keep up the stride quite well.

We boarded a train and the ride was uneventful until we stopped at a summer resort in the mountains. Here, we were permitted to stroll within the station bounds and we stepped into a beautiful area primarily landscaped with bamboo. These are not trees, as we know a tree; each cane comes from the ground and forms a huge group. Some of the canes were all of twelve inches in diameter, with a group up to thirty feet wide. I recalled a song which the family would sing at home, "Where're you walk, tall trees shall fan the glade. Trees where you sit, shall crowd into a shade." With this on my mind, and humming the tune, I re-boarded the train.

Our final destination was close to the Chillilitan airfield, but it was still quite a distance to the camp. Problems started as we moved on. Shoes fell apart, and there was no chance to stop to bind our feet for protection against the searing heat of the road's surface. Occasionally, someone would sit on a tuft of grass to render himself a little first aid, but he was immediately pounced upon and forced onward. Fellows clung together, trying to give each other assistance; others carried or dragged their buddies between them so they could not fall out. Stragglers received the customary treatment from the rifle butt. The human body endured much pain and torture; the miles just came and passed, without any idea of how many.

Some time after darkness that day, we arrived in the worst area thus far encountered. This was known as Camp Makasura. There were long, low, dirty straw and bamboo huts, with doorways at intervals along each side. These were situated under rows of coconut palms. Between the entrances, extending full length, were bamboo shelves about eighteen inches high, upon which we lived and slept. You dared not sit with your feet on the brick path, which ran the full length of the hut, for fear of scorpions that were on occasion seen lurking, close to, or on the brick. One evening, I started to walk toward a doorway when a buddy shouted, "Stop, Bill!" Immediately, I froze. He brought down a wooden clog, crushing a scorpion, at the same time grazing the skin of my little toe, causing a bruise. I limped for a number of days.

The usual routine was carried out here; there was parade at 6:00 a.m., outside of the huts. Japanese guards made a check of our quarters and did a personnel count. Then the fatigues of the day started. I never knew which I preferred: cleaning the latrines caused stomach upheaval equal to the alternative of cleaning out the weevils and maggots from the rice, in preparation for cooking. Those not detailed for latrines the night before were led by the guard into virgin land close by. There, they were compelled to clear it off with their bare hands. A few spades were used to cut the deep roots of small shrubs and briars. The odd tree was pulled over using ropes, with men in tug-of-war fashion. The roots were severed with spades as a trench was dug around the base to weaken the tree's hold.

One evening, after the meager supper, I felt a wave of nausea with a severe toothache. This pain had no comparison to what I encountered a half-hour later. Dr. Dawson (a surgeon, not a dentist) detailed three orderlies to hold me firm while he attached forceps and worked away at the infected tooth. Anesthetic was not available, and the hooked prongs of the root were wrapped around roots of the other teeth, fore and aft. By the time the doctor had managed to break away two of the prongs and unhook the third, also removing the pieces, I was wishing to die. Three days in bed followed; this was an episode I never want repeated.

Back in the newly created garden, I was handed a rake of bamboo about one meter wide. This was used, pulling and pushing, to level off and clean the area in preparation for planting. The cleared area, I estimated, had now reached approximately four acres. Nothing seemed to yield; the weeds held very tightly, in small clumps of clay which were hard to disintegrate, and pieces of root would cling to a prong, which meant more tugging to break it off or pull it out. But finally, a day came when the Japanese drove up in a small truck, full of short, green sticks. Apparently, these were pieces of Tapioca plant which we planted in rows, each piece standing like a sentinel. When the planting was finished, it resembled some pictures captioned, "Lest We Forget."

One morning, we learned this camp was an embarkation base. Ninety Americans, from artillery and navy units, arrived to say they had come to join us, enroute to Japan. With them came a little black terrier dog that answered to the name of Fritz. He matched his masters by displaying every bone in his body, proving he had fared second best in the chow lines. He became a friend of the whole camp, and had a lady friend too. These new arrivals hailed from California, Illinois, New York, North Carolina, West Virginia, Tennessee, Texas, and New Mexico. They were men of the 8th Army, and had surrendered down near Surabaja. The naval men were from two or three surface vessels and one of the American submarines. It was said the sub was unable to surface long enough to charge its batteries, being under the constant surveillance of Japanese surface units, so it was eventually brought to the surface and scuttled.

During that same day, with all men now assembled, we were compelled to complete forms giving our rank and name, home address, military and civilian occupations. All indications of rank having been removed from our clothing, we showed ourselves as AC2s and menial duties men. For civil occupations, we listed vegetable growers, road sweepers, and garbage collectors. When interrogated as to where the RAF technicians were, we told them they were transferred off the island before the Japanese arrived. A second form, demanding allegiance to the Nippon Government, was also signed, but this was covered by our senior officer, in the form of a signed, certified chit (signature under duress), which we each hid for presentation if required after hostilities ceased.

With the appearance of additional guards, we sensed the possible tightening of security measures, so each of us checked our personal belongings in preparation for searches. I had whittled away some time, at Semplak, shaping an early period galleon (like Sir Francis Drake's *Golden Hind*), complete with rigging and figurehead. All component parts had a place in a groove or catched slot within a travel container; complete with my home address inscribed inside the lid. The problem arose as to how to maintain possession; it finished up being buried beneath an officer's cot. Up to this point, the trucks were used to transfer our effects, but from this point on, we had to pack our own, a difficult thing to do without standard equipment. The previous marches had been hard enough for us, without carrying gear. Worse experiences followed.

With no improvement in food, and waistlines slimmer, the Americans killed and ate poor, old Fritz, to give some additional flavour to the unpolished blue rice. Each evening as we stepped outside the hut for roll call, thousands of termites would appear from a hole in the sand and ascend into the beam of the large arc lamp, high up on the compound fence.

Within a few minutes of their ascent each night, darkness fell. Many of them lay dead, next morning, covering large areas beneath the lamps surrounding the camp. A torrential rain would start, followed closely by heavy lighting and thunder. The coconuts would crash down with resounding thuds as they hit the mud or bounced on the hut. This additional water played havoc with the septic tank system; the huge hole dug to receive the normal overflow, would fill and back up. This produced ideal conditions for mosquitoes, and with no suitable materials to combat infestation, we all came under deadly attack within a few days. Consequently, the sick bay received an upsurge in malaria patients, which did nothing to assist the camp morale.

A padre arranged with the new Japanese Commandant to use a marquee-type hut as a church. This was the first opportunity for any of the 242 Squadron's personnel to attend a conducted service since the commencement of hostilities. There were approximately thirty of us, with our heads bowed in prayer as the padre read from the Bible. A guard decided to step inside, but not to join in. No! He was noticed by no one. We first realized his presence when we heard the resounding slap of his hand across the padre's face, and the simultaneous smack of the Bible striking the ground. Then a number of barbaric noises erupted, from what I believe was the ugliest face I had ever seen, as he turned and peered closely into the eyes of each man and slowly made his way among us. We all stood rigidly at attention, without anyone so much as blinking an eye.

Somehow, the padre had vanished (gone to see the Commandant), but he returned, called off the service and made motions that indicated a drunk and feasting man over in the big house. However, this business was ironed out, and routine services commenced (in the form of evening prayer) during the balance of our stay in Chillilitan.

Footwear was a major concern; our boots, or shoes, were in dire need of repair, and materials were non-existent. Wooden clogs, made from old crates cut up with a knife, plus a piece of canvas or cloth for a strap, had to suffice. They were awkward, and difficult to get accustomed to. We didn't know if they could be used to walk any great distance. Fortunately for me, I had purchased a second pair during our days in Batavia because I had lost my kit in Sumatra.

# 16

---

## *The Hell Ship to Singapore*

It was a Sunday morning, quiet and bright, with nature's colours richer than ever before. These were the splendid hues of early morning, and the start of beautiful, clear days. This particular morning will always be remembered, as several of the boys rose early to attend camp church. We sought special prayers and blessings from the padre before stepping out once more onto the hot highway for a long, long march. This was further than the previous ones, requiring much more physical endurance because it did not start before 10:30 a.m. Each man carried only the things he felt able to carry. The fellows that were left behind became heirs to many personal, and treasured, articles. Promises were made that letters, and possibly visitations to each other, would be made after the war, and even the return of one's effects.

It was on this note that many a good pal was separated; the loss to each of us was great. We had become a major part of each other's life, supporting each other, and giving a little boost of encouragement to carry on and endure a lot more. Optimistically, we put as much hope into the Allied positions to the south of us, that they would be strengthened and come to grab us back from these detestable scum. But, when we sat back and were allowed by our partners to meditate upon the situation, it made us realize just how fruitless these hopes were. Men must be given moral support to enable them to fight on, and because we kept ourselves occupied in conversations of reminiscence, or playing chess, bridge or crib, it kept our faculties sound, and alert to the next turn of events.

Once again, the familiar tunes were whistled, which got us off to a good clip along the roads winding through the outskirts of Batavia, toward the docks. As the hours rolled by, the sun poured out its intolerable heat, burning and blistering us into human fritters. We were now being exposed to the native inhabitants as the defeated protectors of their homes and families, but I was convinced they felt something toward us, as they silently watched us pass into oblivion. They, too, had been subjected to slave-labour tactics, which proved to them that the so-called "Asian Liberators" claim, to make Asia for the Asians, was not the case. It was merely the excuse used to exploit and rob them of all essential items needed to assist the Japanese in mastering Asia, and feeding the masses of Japan.

On we trudged. Our shirts were glued to our bodies as if we had just walked out of the ocean, no steady rhythm of marching feet, no whistling. There were a few moans and little talking. No complaining, just retaliatory phrases: "The little bastards—they will pay for this", "I'll kill the first son-of-a-bitch I can lay my hands on when this is all over", and so on. Into the watching crowds, men had thrown certain discards to make their pack lighter. Mine could not be reduced; it was only comprised of a change of shirt and shorts, toothbrush, shaving brush and razor, a few writing materials, knife, fork, spoon, plate and mug, an empty tobacco pouch and pipe, and a thin blanket. This was all tied up in a piece of cloth, in the fashion of a hobo pack. Being a light-footed person, I was still wearing a pair of Oxfords, but doubted they could last much longer.

Gradually, the column filed into the dockyard and onto the same quay that had received us on our arrival in Java. There was no stately ship, just an old freighter with many rusty patches. Just visible were the faces of the Captain, and an army officer, on the bridge. As we approached the gangplank, each man received two loaves of bread, possibly ten ounces each. This was one each for supper and breakfast. I took mine and slowly made my way up onto deck, following the line of fellows across to the opposite side. Not all of the hold's planks were in position, and passing down between them were two canvas chutes, to act as air conductors into the bowels of the tub. At one corner of the hold, a covered staircase led down into a maze of cat walks, built around the hold at one meter levels, down through the boat.

At each level, it looked like shelves, onto which we were rifle-butted like a pack of sheep. This was a Japanese transport, built by rats, for rats. To crawl like a rat was the only way in and out. The butt caught me an unlucky blow on the tip of the shoulder-blade. The nerve-numbing blow left my arm practically paralyzed; thus, I was minus a limb needed for crawling and dragging my pack. I rolled over into position; the loaves now looked the worse for wear, at least what I could see of them as the light had started to draw in very quickly. Somehow, I was supposed to keep a loaf until morning. The problem was how to use my pack as a pillow, and not lie on the bread. Like the fellows around me, and to reduce some of the burden, I ate "supper", thereby leaving only one loaf to take care of. I cannot recall any fellow urinating that evening, in fact from the time of starting out that morning. We were totally dehydrated, through the heat of day, falling asleep with one hand upon the second loaf.

The Dutch fellows were far below on the deck plates, just above the bilge. From this general vicinity, there suddenly broke out a large commotion. At first it was hard to discover what it was all about, until a Dutch officer announced that rats (not two legged ones) were stealing the bread. Naturally, we at such a high location considered our bread would be safe enough, especially as it was inside our pack, with a hand placed on it. However, about two hours had passed when an exceptional weight on my left arm awoke me. Controlling myself, I pulled my muscles taut, lifting and throwing my arm in one motion. The rat was as large as any rabbit I have since handled, and like others that foraged around us, was just too large to be welcomed. The only consolation about the rats was they had not left the ship before we sailed. An old omen states, "Rats will leave a sinking ship before it sails."

The boat pounded along, the engine causing considerable vibration, at no more than five knots. The speed was insufficient to gather enough air in the chutes to keep the temperature down. The place just reeked with sweating bodies and foul air. The only relief came when a good rain cloud passed, but we encountered only three during our five days aboard. Unable to stand or read, we just lay there, sometimes talking a little, but I think most of us were praying that allied subs were afar off. The Captain permitted a ten-minute period, twice a day, for each man to use improvised latrines on the port bow. A section at a time would be ushered in and out by guards. Housed on the forward deck were sick patients, lying under a canvas awning. Most of these were suffering from dysentery. I, like many others, would only urinate during these sessions up on deck. We were only receiving two small meals a day, giving little roughage, so one could hold on. The odd shark was visible in these waters, so we knew the end of any patients that went overboard.

The ship stopped, guttural noises were heard on topside, and slowly we made our way onto the deck to take our first glimpse of Singapore. This was a beautiful harbour. There were many ships, with the whole place bustling and local inhabitants loading supplies for Japan.

After we touched the quayside and formed a group, we were on our way to the east side of the island. The route took us through a section of the city, and I recall two or three beautiful buildings, unscathed from the bombings. Several of the boys, who had been here earlier, pointed out the Pedang and Raffles Hotels. Some of the large apartment blocks had lost part of their upper sections, revealing the small, quaint quarters into which the population was crammed.

Of course, we knew that among the crowds along the roadside there were also traitors. These men, who allowed the Japanese into their country, had stopped the working parties that were assisting in defence projects. If Malaysia was impregnable jungle, as so many British statesmen had claimed, then it would have been isolated enough to have used fire for defensive measures, instead of wasting the lives of men who had become exhausted through constant withdrawals. Everyone knew the ruthless tactics employed by the professional Japanese soldier, and fire would have destroyed the natural sources of food available to them. The native compounds were primitive and would not have been too difficult to relocate. The areas surrounding the landing zones, if burned, would have thwarted jungle warfare and nipped it in the bud, forcing frontal attacks against what little defences had been built over the years. After American oil and steel supplies to Japan had been stopped, it left the Japanese no alternative other than to go to war. Then, it was too late for the allied units to overcome the mistakes.

# 17

## *Change Enroute to Japan*

Neither Singapore nor Pearl Harbour defences were on alert to possible attack. This, I believe, was incompetence, for which thousands suffered. Here were two attacks that should have been Japanese failures, not successes.

We all felt the strain quite quickly. The rest we'd had on the boat was detrimental to us, and the small meals did little to give us strength, stamina, and weight. As we entered the rural area, a road took us across the Kallang Airport, with searing heat bouncing off the runway. The going became extremely difficult, and evidence of past hostilities was revealed. On our left, the huge Changi Jail loomed; its occupants were white women. They shouted and cheered as we passed by. The bars at the windows stood out vividly, in contrast to the white building, pronouncing "prison" in stronger terms than other similar buildings we'd seen elsewhere. Were we headed to such quarters?

Plodding on, jungle-type growth gradually closed in on us. Over water holes, mosquitoes danced in swarms, the occasional one being attracted towards us. Certain areas had been cleared, where now stood rows of white crosses. There were some open holes, and the odd Australian digging, prepared for the future burial of another of his comrades.

Ahead, we saw the barrack blocks of the Changi camp, then heard the distant sounds of a Sergeant Major's voice commanding a company at drill on the barrack square. It was six months or more since the surrender, yet bullshit such as this still ranked high with some of the military fanatics. It was not enough that work parties for the Japanese took their toll; the boys were still subjected to unnecessary drill parades. One could only suppose that they wanted us to work off the little nourishment we received from Red Cross supplies.

Eventually, we came to a halt on the same bit of tarmac in the square, and no one could dispute that we certainly did look like rats, compared with our army counterpart. Camp playing fields were on the opposite side of the road. It was here on the cricket pitch, under canvas and immediately in front of the pavilion, that we slept off the agonizing pain. Two days later, the Japanese guards (complete with their bicycles) took us down the road, to open up another section of the jungle. We were a small contingent of some three hundred men. The area designated for clearing would just about house a grave for each of us. Who knew if we were not clearing it for this purpose?

Small, red, armbands were given to us. This enabled the guards to keep close tabs on what they considered was a technical group, enroute to Japan. Meanwhile, with ropes lashed to the upper parts of the trees and axes striking at the roots, the boys toppled them one by one. Mattocks, shovels, picks, and bare hands gradually removed the roots and other types of vegetation from the soil. Each day, you could see that the jungle carpet had been rolled back a little further. Each night, the boys returned to the improvised showers, which helped to cool them down, but did little to remove the grime. Soap was unobtainable, and the days when we last used any were long forgotten.

I became the quartermaster for the group, and with two AC2s, we made a daily trip to the barracks main store. The Red Cross had already brought in large supplies of food, clothing, and footwear. Fortunately for us, we received much needed supplies to help sustain the force. The army quartermaster sympathized with us, and held a clothing parade, which enabled us to discard our rags. We became respectably clothed again. Each man received a dead soldier's battle dress, with a Red Cross pair of boots. This kindness gave our morale a much-needed boost to face the unknown winter conditions of Japan.

During these days on Singapore, we were able to help the army divisions consume a large quantity of Australian and New Zealand mutton. Apparently, the huge freezers, that held a two-year supply for England, had started to thaw out. Japanese bombing had destroyed the freezing plant. This type of nourishment did much to improve the general condition of many, and we especially needed it when marching and digging.

My eyes began to give me a lot of trouble. This meant a trip from the zone of our encampment, across the Australian sector, to the hospital. Between zones there were areas designated as no-man's-land. The only way to cross these was to form columns of four, and march through with two officers at the head, carrying some type of banner. At the halfway point, we received a command of "eyes right", thus saluting a guard (not Japanese, but one of our so-called allies, the Sikhs), possibly those who were traitors to Malaysia's lines of defence. Any infraction on this march would find these same people enforcing punishment. We heard that several of these guards were secretly disposed of by their fellow countrymen, the Gurkhas. They stealthily pounced on them and knifed them, in complete silence; they are famed for never drawing their knives without drawing blood.

I arrived in the Aussie camp and spoke with several fellows, making new friends while inquiring about the correct way to the base hospital. One man, in particular, interested me, sitting at a little table, sharpening scalpels. He was a good friend of the surgeons, as he kept their instruments in top shape. While we spoke in the hall, the sound of a chisel could be heard coming through the open, double doors a few feet away. However, the chisel was not working on stone, but on the kneecap of a soldier. When I glanced through the door, I saw the surgical brace and bit at work in the competent hands of an army surgeon. There were five surgeons in all, helping to pin the knee and place a plate, which would stiffen the leg forever. I found a General Practitioner, who diagnosed my trouble as malnutrition and gave me a daily ration of Marmite. As the days rolled by, I became better acquainted with the Australians as I passed back and forth to obtain this ration. During these days, we watched (with grave concern) companies of men being marched away. They were departing for Thailand, to help in the building of the railroad to Burma. Here, the Japanese were going to use white slave labour. Years earlier, the British had refused to build such a railway because the number of native's lives lost would be far too great. Yet, during these dark days, men were marched off to a death from cholera, within the unknown jungle.

Our small group spent roughly six weeks on the island of Singapore, and for six weeks the boys laboured with the swamp vegetation, revealing the rich leaf-mould from centuries passed. The waste foliage had been burned, leaving the area bare. In the jungle, the dark, moldy odours were nauseating, and the humid heat, suffocating and tiring. Only after several hours did the days work cease. It was almost impossible to strike a stride, to carry ourselves back to camp.

The improvised showers were somewhat refreshing, but you dared not rinse your mouth, or drink the water because it was not chlorinated (its origin unknown). About eighty percent of the boys were addicted to smoking, and with tobacco out of the question, they chose to dry several different types of leaves. Papers, too, were not available; many good books had pages torn out in order to roll up a substitute cigarette. This combination created a peculiar taste, and many sore throats. I did not partake of any such concoction.

What monotony! The daily routine was consistently repeated, with the same menu daily, and possibly to eternity. There was no happier day than the day when we were told to pack. We were leaving the Changi abode, perhaps a little stronger because of the mutton.

*My father's home in Nethercott, Tackley, Oxford-shire, where he was born. It survived the War of the Roses in 1644—June 1–2. A definite record of Nethercott dates back to 1346.*

*November 1919*

*My mother—Florence Bridge—1917*

*William Alfred Franklin: Born, Sept 29, 1919.*

*A group of the Boy's Brigade. First Oxford Company—1932*

*William Franklin, September 1, 1939*
*(At mobilization)*

*Boys Brigade Soccer Team Season champions*
*1935–36 (back row—third from right)*

*Shrapnel that singed my hair, 1940*

*On a spare parts collection mission from a mainte-nance unit, 1940*

*Buddies after Dutch capitulation Java march, 1942*

*The Squdron Emblem, 1941*

*Number given upon arrival at Nagasaki—Dec. 8, 1942*

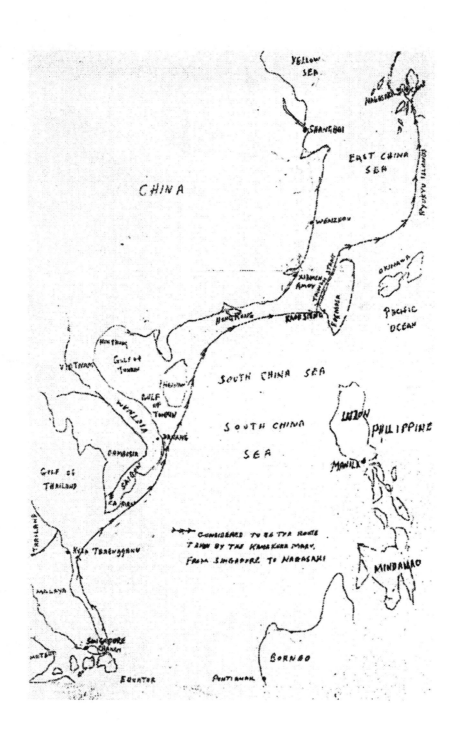

*4,000 ex-P.O.W.s were aboard from the Philipines to British Columbia en-route home.*

*This is about what the Nagasaki bomb looked like when I saw it explode over the city August 9, 1945 at 11:02 am—the time is accurate; it was recorded by a watch stopped by the explosion—Walter Bantin, wireless operator of 242.*

*USS Aircraftt Carrier "Chenango", which took us from Nagasaki to Okinawa, September 1945. On route a floating mine just missed the stern, and we had a five-day encounter with a typhoon, which packed winds of 180 mph.*

*"Ile de France"—Halifax to Southhampton with 4,000 ex-P.O.W.s. Arrived November 3, 1945.*

*Our parent's golden wedding, 1968*

*Marjorie at the gate to our new home, 1943*

*"Jodi" and I after purchasing our store, July 1946*

*My sisters, Ruth & Mary (at left), with my brother Leonard's wife, Ollie.*

*With brother Len, Uncle Fred and cousin George, 1946*

*Jean Mair, sister of Ollie Franklin*

*Slim and his wife Gena—1990. Slim helped me after an accident at the dockyard.*

*My daughter, Rosalind and sons, David and Ian*

*With Ralph Kelm at a lumber grading championship, 1976*

*With John Ramsay, who retired with me on September 21, 1984*

*Phyllis and Ian*

# Romance on a Sunday

*Celebration mood . . . diamond wedding couple Mr and Mrs Marsland*

A COUPLE who met at Sunday School in Manchester were celebrating their diamond wedding anniversary today.

Tom and Jeanie Marsland, who live at Glebe House, in Mill Street, Kidlington, moved to Oxford after their wedding and first lived in Cowley.

Mr Marsland worked as a laboratory technician at the University Physiology Department until his retirement in 1978.

Mrs Marsland was a teacher at Donnington Infant School, and later at East Oxford Infant School, where she was deputy head.

The couple were members of Temple Cowley United Reform Church, where they taught in the Sunday School.

They moved to Glebe House in 1988.

*Bill Frankliun today: a woodworker and gardener who has elevated the lifelong hobbies to an art form. Happily retired in the rural seclusion of south-east Aldergrove, Franklin devotes many hours to building beautiful dollhouses, cabinets and furniture, as well as maintaining a floral display in his yard that is the envy of many neighbours.*

*Bill Franklin survived a brutal two years and eight-months as a prisoner of war in Nagasaki, as well as the A-bomb that was dropped on the city on August 9, 1945. He's holding the International Prisoners of War medal he recently received, inscribed with the words, "Intrepid Against All Adversity". Franklin will attend a special ceremony at Aldergrove Legion's cenotaph on Sunday, August 13, to commemorate the 50th Anniversary of V-J Day—the allied forces' victoriy over the last Axis power holdout. —Kurt Langmann photo*

*The squadron emblem. Left to right: Erice Ball, Douglas Bader and William McKnight. Ball had just received the D.F.C., Bader the D.S.O. and McKnight a bar to his D.F.C.*

John Gordon

**Bill Franklin, superintendent of the recent Langley Garden Club and Horitcultural Society's 12th annual spring flower show, photographs entries at St. Joseph's Church.**

# 18

---

## *To Nagasaki*

November 29, 1942, was a bright Sunday morning and the day designated for us to leave Singapore for Japan. Six weeks had passed since our arrival at the Changi camp. During this time, several of the boys had been hospitalized due to malaria and dysentery. The water was so poor that the maximum chlorine was used, and it was boiled before one dared to drink it. Personal hygiene was extremely difficult to maintain because very little soap was available. The sweat and grime stuck to us like glue.

We had to be constantly vigilant that our hands were kept well clear of our food and mouth. Two cauldrons of water were kept boiling at all times. This allowed us to immediately sterilize the utensils we used for eating and preparing food. After being sterilized, they were kept wrapped in muslin cloth to keep the flies off. Eating was a ritual, and if anyone failed to protect his rations properly and ate food touched by a fly, he found himself in hospital the next day with dysentery.

During our stay, several men had contracted that dreaded disease. The only relief came from drinking lightly brewed tea, heavily sugared. With the medical orderly, I would visit these fellows in the hospital. They could only lay and wait for the next call for the toilet, until they were too weak to answer the call. They died with excruciating pain, indescribable to those who have never experienced it. Those of us remaining never knew if we would be next to enter into a six foot plot in the newly cleared land.

Our small contingent (now less than three hundred) fell in on parade, with one lone, British army officer in charge. Half a dozen Japanese army guards rode up on bicycles. At the command, "Joski", we were counted and our armbands checked. "Tidadi mckay tidadi". We turned right as ordered, marched off the old cricket pitch, and headed for the naval docks east of the Changi camp.

The area we entered had been called the "Impregnable Bastion of the Pacific", and "Gateway to the East", but all we saw were a number of empty quaysides, with empty warehouses between. There was no evidence that it was a naval establishment, or of any damage from hostilities. We came to a halt beside one of the quays. A small tender came alongside, and we embarked. Two or three other vessels followed, and soon there was a small flotilla heading out into the Strait of Singapore toward the Japanese boat, which was not visible from this point.

Slim Lodge said to Reg Malkin, "I wonder what sort of a bucket they're going to put us in this time?" "If it's anything like the one from Java, it may as well sink here before sailing!" he replied. I added, "It's probably complete with two little loaves of bread and a compliment of rats ready to steal them again!"

As the tender came around the end of the quay, we were spellbound, absolutely speechless at what we saw lying ahead. There was a light camouflage-gray, long boat with beautiful, sleek lines, very modern in appearance. It made a lovely silhouette against the sunlit, emerald-green shoreline across the strait of Singapore.

As we approached, details were revealed: portholes, promenade deck railings, with lounge windows behind and situated below the lifeboat deck. Also, it had twin funnels set at a pleasing angle. Two flights of boarding steps had been lowered, one at midship, and the other aft, where we boarded. The stern had two decks: the lower one had an auxiliary steering unit, and the upper deck resembled a captain's walk, open and railed like the promenade deck.

Naval guards directed us toward stairs on the port side, which took us up onto the promenade deck. With high expectations, hopes of being accommodated in one of the lounge areas were soon dashed, as we discovered we would remain on this open deck throughout the voyage to Japan. Each man, in turn, staked out sufficient space in which to lie down and sleep. I, like most of the others, had so little in the way of personal belongings, that my small bundle was carried under one arm. I was very grateful to the army stores captain, who had made the battle dress uniforms and Red Cross boots available to us! Without them, the cold nights would have stricken us.

I never forgot my father's advice, "Be sure to keep your greatcoat on hand at all times. It's your best friend." Ironically, I had lost it the moment hostilities started at Palembang, which prevented us from returning to base before fleeing south, back to Java. I wished wholeheartedly that I had it now!

Orders were given that we had to remain lying down on the deck, and we would receive food only twice a day. On the main deck, "Benjo" (toilets) were set up under canvas, near the stern. One sat over a pole and an open trough of running water. Washing was not permitted. Apparently, all interior space was occupied with Japanese officers and men returning to Japan, on leave, except for two men: General Heath, Joint Commander of British Forces in Singapore, and his batman.

At half past four in the afternoon, a detail of men descended to the kitchen to get our meal, rice and cabbage soup. They passed by the ship's plaque and were able to read some of the statistics. These details were passed on to us as they ladled out the food. This boat had been prefabricated in Harland and Wolfe dock yards in Belfast, Ireland, shipped in their own ships, and assembled in Japan. A liner of some 23 thousand tons, with oil turbines and capable of twenty-seven knots, she was named *Kama Kura Maru*.

# 19

*Running the Gauntlet*

Shortly after we had finished eating, the ship's telegraph started ringing, and a slight throbbing was felt as the engines began to turn. More rings; the donkey engines tugged on chains that clanged as they brought up the anchor. We started gliding eastward as the engines eased us onto a course in the middle of the strait, heading toward the northern part of the archipelago. The Dutch East Indies archipelago is comprised of some 20,000 islands.

Since we were only one or two degrees north of the equator, daylight came to an abrupt end as the sun sank below the horizon. This sudden change into night brought with it a drastic drop in temperature. With the breeze created by the ship's movement, we began to feel cold. Luckily for most of our contingent, we were forward of the open railing and enjoyed a measure of protection due to the solid gunwale. However, it was little consolation to me, having only a thin sheet, which I doubled and wrapped around me.

Lying on the wooden deck was not comfortable, and the little bundle I was using for a pillow, developed hard spots, which dug into my face. One by one, we all became a disgruntled bunch, but knew it would be hopeless to complain. Morton, my neighbour, had a scratchy old blanket, but it did give a little more protection than my flimsy cover, so I suggested pooling our resources, to which he agreed. My flannel sheet gave relief from the rough blanket, which in turn seemed to seal in the heat generated by our bodies. It worked out well; we slept soundly for a number of hours, waking at daybreak.

Gradually, everyone got up for a stretch, cussing the conditions under which we were being transported. Each gave vent to their feelings, that they would like to massacre the little bastards! Morton and I told those around us how we had coped, and soon other groups began huddling together, sharing blankets.

General Heath and two guards stepped over the threshold of a cabin door, and proceeded down to the main deck. He carried a soap dish and towel. One of the guards handed him a wooden bowl and some cold water. Stripped to his waist, he washed and then returned to the cabin. All communication between the General and us was prohibited.

"Meal one" was served around 9 a.m., with the prospect of a good day ahead, weatherwise at least. The ship was slicing the water with a slight swishing sound, moving along at a fair clip. The engines, humming with little vibration, gave a smooth ride on a moderate sea. The captain stayed on a course parallel to the shoreline, and after the sun climbed above the morning haze, it gave us a good view of the terrain beyond. It appeared heavily treed, and visibility became so good we could observe the movement of natives within small compounds. The captain maintained his course along the shore of Malaysia, to a point close to Kula Trengganu. Here, he changed direction to cross the mouth of the Gulf of Thailand (Siam), to a point close to Ca Mau, South Vietnam. The scenery was magnificent and the water very clear, and for three days a large shark, with a pilot fish at his nose, followed along the port side. The weather was excellent for a cruise, but being compelled to stay in bed, we found excuses to walk to the bridge and peer over the railing.

Another course change was made, crossing the Gulf of Tonking, to run alongside Hainan. We headed across the South China Sea to arrive in early morning fog at Kaohsiung, Formosa (now Taiwan). Here, General Heath and his batman left us. He whispered as he passed, "Don't let them get you down. Chins up!" and he descended to the tender.

We crossed the East China Sea, and began to feel the cold now as the wind swept across our bow, until we entered sheltered waters, passing a few small islands and into Nagasaki. The voyage had taken eight days. In the failing light, we could see the area was quite industrial. We left the *Kama Kura Maru,* and boarded a multi-decked ferry that took us across the bay to a dockyard, by the entrance to the open sea. The night shifts were working in several areas, as the resounding hammering of riveter's guns rang out. It was obvious to us; this was where we would be forced to work, right on a military target.

We were marching on the last leg of the journey from the hot, hostile tropics into the cold, damp evening, with its setting sun. As we passed through the dockyard toward the camp, it seemed as if every movement of the past year had taken place according to a well-organized plan. This December 8, 1942, one year to the day on which we had sailed from Glasgow, Scotland, we arrived as scheduled. The *Kama Kura Maru* became much sought after by the American Naval Forces, and was finally caught and sunk by the submarine *U.S.S. Gudgeon,* on April 28, 1943.

Outside the dockyard gates, in a small cluster, stood a group of dismal looking buildings which included a small hospital, a store, and offices. Then a foundry loomed up on the left, with its huge pile of scrap iron and salvaged pieces, which had dropped from the many drills throughout the boats. Women of the Ladies Corps volunteered to the call of Tojo's wife, "Get out and help the cause by day, meet the large transports, and entertain the boys by night." They swept the dirt and waste material, from the bilge to the upper decks. They carried this rubbish in two flat baskets, one attached at each end of a pole, across their shoulders. The girls came down the scaffolding planks to a huge dump, where others sat picking out all the minute pieces of metal, to be added to the corroded pile at the foundry.

Next, came a small yard. At first, we thought it was a lumberyard, but peering deeply, we could see the old, skillful, boat builder at work. A fine, shapely, submarine chaser was being built of wood. We watched this from day to day for several months. Finally, with a coat of gray paint, with a red-bottomed hull, she was ready to take to the water.

The road beyond this area was close to the water, with a high cliff of sandstone on its right. Gangs of men were drilling into this rock, while captive Koreans filled carts with the broken pieces, ran them down to the water's edge on trucks, and dumped the contents into the water. On their return trips, the workers would alternately drop off at a small hut, and pick up a dime. Working in pairs, these fellows gradually built up a rhythm that helped them make many trips a day. This development made tremendous progress each month, reclaiming land from the sea by tipping in their small loads of fill.

A naval barracks stood beyond the drilling area, behind which a small population was housed. After a march of approximately two miles, we passed through a small gully where the camp was situated, down behind a bluff. The guards hustled us into rooms on the seaward side, sixty to each room. I was in room #20. These rooms were fitted with a double bunk bed, extending full-length down each side of the room, like shelving. They had straw-matting covers (no ceiling), with double-glazed doors. There were tables down the centre, with forms on either side, and a locker for the chinaware stood under the window, at the opposite end to the door.

In the centre of the concrete floor was a small pit for a fire. This was never used, nor was heat ever supplied. Beneath the bunks was damp soil, enclosed with sliding doors. Within this so-called cupboard, we were supposed to store our working clothes and boots. At no time were we permitted the use of our boots outside of work at the yard. During the hours spent in camp, we were compelled to wear wooden clogs without socks. Roll call, on the first evening, was exceptionally long. A Dutch interpreter explained the orderly NCO's desire to express his wishes for our happy stay, and welcomed us to Japan. Then the standing camp orders were read.

The only occasions for leaving your room were for visits to the toilet, or sick bay. There was no visiting of the other rooms, and no smoking until permission was granted. When leaving a room, one must wear his topcoat, but it must never be worn to the dockyard, where one required additional warmth; it was strictly denied. Spittoons, placed on either side of the doorway, were to be cleaned every day. Here, we all agreed that a detailed man each week would attend to this, but if any man used them, the user would be responsible. Occasionally, a guard would use it, just to be a bloody nuisance.

The rule was "No one will wash, other than his hands." Washing facilities were in the courtyard; only cold water was provided. The heads (toilets), called the "benjo", were housed in a long shed. They were open holes (with lid covers) inside small compartments, built over a large concrete tank. Smoking was not permitted. All guards were to be saluted if you were wearing a hat, otherwise, stop and bow. Lights were to be out at 9 p.m., reveille at 5 a.m. Five minutes prior to bedtime, and after rising in the morning, everybody had to remove all clothing and scrub himself with a round, pot brush attached to strings. This was to be pulled vigorously over the torso to stimulate circulation, at the same time curtailing colds and sickness. Everyone had to respond immediately; fatigues were handed out if you did not vacate your bed at the first strains of the bugle. We would nudge each other to ensure we would not be caught.

Our personal belongings were searched. No pens, pencils, paper, knife, fork, or spoon could be kept. A couple of chessboards, crib boards, and two or three decks of cards were all we had left for pleasure. At the warning bugle for roll call, all ashtrays were collected and cleaned. Personally, I was not a smoker, but the shortage of food compelled me to start. The smoker's body did not demand edibles to the same degree as the one who did not smoke. This proves smoking to be a deterrent to good health, since it lessens the need for consumption of good, wholesome food, and impregnates the lungs with smoke. However, it did save me the demoralizing effect of consistently walking around with a feeling of hunger. So, like the others,

I accepted and smoked part of the ration of five a day, keeping the remainder to trade for extra food. Lighting up after consuming breakfast, lunch, and three times after supper, we were like pieces of automatic machinery, adding another glow of light to an illuminated window.

# 20

---

## *Camp Fukuoka*

Rooms #1 to #5 were occupied by Dutch and British sailors who had survived naval engagements, their ships being either sunk or scuttled. Three Dutch hospital ships were seized at sea and the doctors placed in various camps. It was from these earlier arrivals that we ascertained how conditions and treatment were working out.

The *H.M.S. Exeter* and *H.M.S. Perth* were just two of the dozen or so boats lost around the Dutch East Indies. On various occasions I rubbed shoulders with some of these boys, and learned of their resentments. They spoke of their displeasure with the upper echelon of the Allied Fleet. Reports had always been favourable, indicating that International Manoeuvres were a total success. At no time was it ever considered a necessity that the basic fighting equipment of the Allies should be interchangeable, and never before had this need been more vital than in the closing days of the Dutch East Indies Campaign.

At lunch one day, sitting apart from the group, a sailor from the cruiser *H.M.S. Exeter* told of their last encounter with enemy ships. They were in Surabaya (on the northeast coast of Java), trying to find ammunition, especially 8" shells. Unfortunately, she was obliged to sail without any, as only metric stocks were available. What a disaster! The *Exeter* escorted by destroyers *H.M.S. Encounter* and the *U.S.S. Pope*, tried to escape through the Sunda Straits and head for the Indian Ocean. The only chance the Captain had was to make a dash for the open waters, away from the Japanese fleet, but the attempt failed. Units of His Majesty's Fleet were bottled up; they fought until the ammo was spent, scuttled the boats, and took to the rafts, and one lifeboat for officers and captain. Many of the boys had no where to go. Their only recourse was to jump into the sea, inflate their lifejacket, and pray for a quick pick-up.

They banded together as closely as possible; the Japanese fleet had sailed out of sight. Sharks were swimming all around the perimeter of the floating sailors. Enemy aircraft appeared and flew low over their heads, with guns blazing. Some were hit, and a few killed. The worst thing possible had occurred; blood was now flowing in the water, and the sharks were roused. Immediately, the men were detailed to beat the water at alternating intervals to keep the marauders away. One by one, the wounded were assisted into the boat for attention by the doctor. Night fell quickly, and those in the boat, or on the rafts, rotated with those in the water. This was done approximately every hour, due to the cold once the sun had gone down.

Twenty-four hours passed before a Japanese destroyer came to pick up officers only, but when they refused to leave the men, the boat left. After another twenty-four hours, the same request was made, but this time there was no response from the water. Later, planes appeared, strafing on two or three more occasions. Numbers had been quietly diminishing even without these murderous acts taking their toll. The boat was now punctured. Water gradually took it down until it capsized, taking the seriously wounded men with it. There was nothing to eat for seventy hours, and many stomachs were emptied through retching from the intake of salt water polluted with oil. They struggled to stay afloat and alive.

Finally, after seventy-two hours, the Japanese destroyer returned for the third time, and picked up all survivors. There were 104 British men of all ranks, plus the survivors from the *Pope*. We had been in complete ignorance of this development, which occurred on March 1, and had continued according to plans. Early on Sunday morning, March 8, 1942, *H.M.S. Exeter* had been due to rendezvous with the R.A.F. Fighter Wing at Tjilajap on the south coast of Java.

While sitting at the table trying to eat and contain a bowl of rice with a few little fish cooked into a watery, vegetable stew, we could hear the water lapping against the wall beneath the window. Only then did we realize how recently this area had been reclaimed from the sea. On the ensuing days, the Koreans worked hard, pushing the waterline farther and farther back, making an area large enough to house an additional barrack building, bath house, garden and parade ground. This also included a strip beyond the fence, which became a road two years later.

The sun was still quite high in the sky, its warmth a welcome relief from the cold sea breezes experienced one week ago. A head popped through the doorway and requested that we should all make our way into the inner courtyard, at the sound of the bugle. When everybody had assembled, the Japanese interpreter announced the arrival of a high-ranking Japanese officer, a member of the royal household. He informed us that if we behaved ourselves and worked diligently for the Nippon Government, it might be possible for us to return home to our loved ones. He considered it would be in ten years time. During the intervening years, we were to work in the dockyard, producing ships so that Red Cross parcels could be brought to us. We were to assist in building larger docks because after Japan had won the war they would take over the shipbuilding industry of the world.

At this point, a tremendous roar of laughter expelled from every one of us. Guards suppressed it rapidly with a few hasty face slaps. Our visitor then expressed his view of our ignorance toward someone who had come all the way from Tokyo to welcome us to Japan. As our friend, he was conveyor of the good news; if you work hard, you might get home one fine day.

On the morrow, we marched down to an area (later known among us as Boys Town) where we had our first experience with the Kigoon (Japanese sailor). It was here we learned it was their official capacity to convey us into the dockyard; guards of both services were to patrol the yard. The gestapo police controlled the civilian foremen, who were responsible for our production within the yard. Interpreters had been selected to work with each department, and on this first day some choice of jobs was given to us. Like most of the others, I had never been into a dockyard, and lacked the knowledge of trade grouping. However, ships carpenter sounded inviting enough to give it a whirl. We were a small group, and the first words our Japanese interpreter said were, "When are the God-dam Yanks going to fetch us out of here?" Without showing too much enthusiasm, we asked where he was from, and we learned that he was born in Tacoma, Washington, USA.

In the late thirties, the Japanese Government promoted tours of Japan for children of Japanese families, born in the United States. Their caption was "Visit your Fatherland; come and see what your parents have left behind". A tour consisted of passage there and back, with a conducted trip through the islands. When they arrived at Yokohama, government officials collected their passports, to be returned after the tour. Later, questions were asked about how they had enjoyed it, what they had seen, and their opinions of the country. To show appreciation and courtesy to the officials, they replied affirmatively; it was a good trip and a nice country. To this response, they were politely told, "You like Japan, so you can stay and fight for it."

To meet an ally was a great up-lift, and made us feel that we had at least one friend in this alien land. Like us, his aim was to stay out of trouble, do as little as possible, and return back home. After this brief introduction, he led our small party along a partially built highway to meet the civilians of our group. Enroute to a small wooden enclosure, built between the concrete pillars which formed part of the dock's superstructure, we passed a small group of men mixing small quantities of sand, gravel, and cement in a little tray. This mixture, when ready, was tipped to form a part of the new road being built through the centre of the dockyard. The methods of production were a terrific strain on the men, who tried hard to accomplish so much more than what was humanly possible. If they succeeded in completing more today than yesterday, that amount of new work was the expected target, per day, thereafter. Yet, they were fools enough to strive for extra footage, regardless of the outcome.

While waiting for our interpreter, close to the small shack, we watched Dutch ex-navy personnel perform their task of plate welding. These plates, thin and of soft metal, were being shaped into bulkheads, and would be dropped by crane into their respective locations within the ships. Later, we as ships carpenters, complete with wire hawsers, turnbuckles, spanners, nuts, bolts and washers, would pull these bulkheads forward and aft, lining them up for interlocking with their component parts of deck beams and bilge members. Or, they were pulled to port and starboard, for locking into the hull plates.

Five men emerged from a small wooden door, wearing armlets with red bands (from one to three) which denoted their seniority. Three bands indicated the chief, a man of substantial stature, who grunted and plodded around like an old sow. During the time I was to work under his jurisdiction, I found him quite harmless. The next two, with whom we accomplished most of the work, could speak a few words of English. In their own manner, they tried to show sympathy, and also related their experiences with the navy during World War I; for a time, they were on a British ship. These two turned out to be quite affable and congenial.

The afternoon visit came to a close. The new camp residents had found work, without trouble, on the first trip to the yard. The outlook was grim with winter approaching. How strong and furious would it be? We had no idea. It was obvious, however, that many a long, cold day around steel was in store; how would we dress? How could we stay warm? Supper that night was soybean-paste-flavoured soup, thickened with a little flour, and cut "digon" (a vegetable the shape of a parsnip and with the taste of turnip, extra bitter) served with rice. This became our regular evening meal for several months.

Small wooden boxes (complete with a flat lid) containing two compartments, the larger for a rice ration and the other for unflavoured digon, were supplied to each person, for lunch purposes only. These were packed while a breakfast of rice, with hot green tea, was being eaten around six in the morning. Some six hours later, a cold, cold lunch was eaten from your personalized little box. It was washed out another six hours later, smelling sour after arriving back at camp. Wash the box, and not yourself, was the order of the day. If you washed, you might catch a cold, and become sick and unable to work. Becoming sick, and obliged to stay at camp, would reduce your rations by one-half, providing you were able to work in camp. If confined to bed, your ration was reduced to one-third; as the old cliché states, "If ye can't work, we can't keep ye."

# 21

---

## *Slaves to the Dockyard*

Those early days in Japan were cold. Each morning, the guards would take a count of each group leaving the room to work at the docks, then march us down to the naval barrack in the public square. This was where the fun started. While we stood at attention in the freezing winds blowing off the China Sea, the navy and army personnel, plus the gestapo, would try to count us before we proceeded to the dockyard. It seemed as if they counted our feet, multiplied by four (we were in columns of four), and then divided by two; but somehow, they never agreed. The headcounters, using bead slides (an abacus), would slide beads, and then drop them back for a restart. They would try again, for a second and third time, without a common result. Meanwhile, we were all standing there freezing to death; the small amount of clothing each man possessed gave inadequate protection. Our topcoats were left in camp, neatly folded on our beds, miles away.

Some days, thirty to forty-five minutes were lost on this stupid count. To get the blood circulating again, we moved forward at the double. As soon as we were dismissed to our various groups, everyone made a beeline to stand around the riveter's braziers. We would catch a little of the radiated heat, and the coke fumes would start a pandemonium of coughing. Unfortunately for my group, in those early days we were assigned to the bowels of ships where little riveting was being done. Consequently, a number of the boys soon contracted colds, which developed into pneumonia. By the end of that first Easter, 1943, approximately sixty had died.

The two civilians I worked with moved cautiously and with an air of confidence. They had the job masterfully mapped out, stage by stage, and as each ship took shape, our duties were performed with a minimum of effort. We would tighten a hawser here, or slacken off there, and the plumb bob would swing over the previously marked plumb lines.

In this way, our small group gradually lined up the boat from stem to stern. We started with the bow stem, then the stern post. The main bulkheads were next, followed by a number of hull plates (which were shored in by poles and wedges and driven home by another segment of our group), hull ribs, and main deck beams, to tie in the sides. Lower deck beams, within the holds, were temporarily placed, with a bolt into a rib and support from one of our poles. This was a precarious situation, as they swayed until the deck plates were lowered in and placed on them, giving stability before raising the main deck beams around the holds. They, also, were given support from poles, to enable deck work to proceed.

The placing of so many loose ribs, with plates just floating on them, made it very difficult to line up each beam. The men working on top of the deck plates would scream for a beam to be lined up to their holes in the plates so they could put in a temporary bolt, and give some support to others. They could not do this until we had lined up all the beams beneath them, systematically. With the sudden addition of so many parts, we were kept busy plumbing up and leveling off, using saws, wedges, poles and sledge hammers. It was interesting work if one was working for his livelihood, but for the likes of us, who were barely existing, it was too much of a chore.

Our group of four was taken to a stack of poles, which were used to shove in the hull plates. The top ends averaged six inches in diameter, with butt ends from twelve to sixteen inches diameter. Some were better than forty feet long. Reg and Frisby were placed at the small end, while (for some unknown reason) Slim and I always received the large end. Actually, they were trees, and heavy! This was a task, but we did lift, with a little assistance, and carried the poles between two to three hundred yards, to the end of a dock. Due to the weight, we did not hold them for lowering into the dock; we stood and heaved them in, and on occasion, the odd one would crack or break like a matchstick

We went down under the boat, and after making a notch for a piece of angle-iron plate (which was placed at the top to take the pressure as the pole was lifted and wedged into position), we hoisted each pole into position. The most difficult sections were around the contours at the stern and poop deck. When such a task was completed, the civilian foreman gave us a little yasme (rest). We would group ourselves in a quiet area beneath the boat.

One tubby Japanese 17 year-old always carried a piece of chalk, to use when we sat around in a small group. Invariably, he would draw pictures depicting the Navy or Airforce, adding a few digits here and there, which emphasized the progress of German operations in Europe. On one such occasion, I took his chalk and drew a picture of a large, conventional-type bomb on the hull of the boat above us. I wrote the number twenty thousand pounds along it. I then told him to watch carefully, because one day such a bomb would be dropped on Nagasaki, and that would be kaput (the finish), which he understood.

We were lifting poles, pulling block and tackle ropes, twisting turn-buckles, and swinging hammers, all on a handful of rice, aiding these barbarians against our fellow countrymen. No, this was not for us. Whenever the opportunity arose, these previously executed chores would gradually be altered. Two or three turns of a buckle would cause a gap between plate and beam, and knocking loose a wedge would drop the pole causing a dip in the deck.

Later, some of the men doing the plating appeared, carrying a wooden pattern. The plater's foreman became mad as a March Hare because beams and plates stood out of line. The patterns proved that the degrees of curve and line in the beams were good. Our own Chief Pig, nostrils enlarged ten times, started to rave because our work was now off-centre. It was all in vain to shout and stamp, because the added weight was now such that it became impossible to pull, jack, or shore these units back to where they should be. There had been too great a time lapse.

In the lower sections, small adjustments had been made; a second reaming of rivet holes had thrown these plates off permanently. Consequently, a little patchwork job was necessary at the main deck level.

Naturally, the required strength and stability had been lessened, the defects being plugged with strips of scrap, and wedges, welded in. This also caused caulking problems at the seams. The riveters could not help as the rivets were too short, and in some cases snapped off as they cooled down; thus, more welding was involved. Finally, the poop deck, plus wheelhouse and stern-quarters, were set up. This closed off our group, for this boat.

A few problems had arisen beneath the forward part of a hull in dry-dock #1. I was one assigned to go and work under this thing. The cramped conditions made it almost impossible to swing a hammer. Under the main keel plate, a riveter had removed too many blocks in a single run, allowing the plate to sit a full inch from the bilge beams. The foreman gestured for us to proceed, a simple job of raising blocks back into position, and then we could take a rest. The topmost block of each stack, or position, had been cut to shape so that it would cradle the contour of the plate. We made a real meal of this job, with poles, jacks, wedges, blocks, swinging hammers, wedges breaking, and poles splitting; plates and beams never came together again.

The Japanese chargehand with us explained that his friend, a welder, would come to our rescue, so we hid ourselves while he vanished to fetch him. At first, they couldn't agree, but then our Japanese boy, the chargehand, promised he would pay for his friend's next visit to the brothels in Nagasaki. Once again, the welder (using scrap metal) patched up a defect, and the boat was launched a week later, with a bulge in the keel plate. After launching on Monday, the Japanese chargehand, (smiling and exposing a mix of rotten and gold teeth) explained he had no money left. He continued to tell us that his wife was pregnant, so in keeping with Japanese tradition, he had not slept with his wife since the date of conception. Instead, men, with wives in confinement, would patronize the various establishments found in the cities. The past week-end had cost him too much for himself leaving him unable to keep his promise to his friend, the welder.

# 22

##### —

## *Sickness, Little Food, & Cold, Cold, Cold.*

With number one dry-dock empty, our group moved into number three; this was a different picture, in the working conditions and the grim prospects ahead. Here, I first encountered the usefulness of the adze, being given the task of shaping the top block for one of the tiers. It is a fascinating tool, requiring a fair amount of skill to use it correctly, and to come up with the desired product. Water seepage was a big problem for us in this dock, causing us to work in water for countless days on end, as we restaged the blocks readying them for the next keel to be laid.

The treacherous winds off the China Sea were now colder, with greater velocity. Our body weight had been reduced to approximately half of what it was when taken prisoner. This alone had weakened our resistance to the cold, and with such small meals and no protein, malnutrition began to take its toll. Many of us were experiencing degrees of beriberi, affecting the legs to a point where several men collapsed. Pressure on one's legs left indentations in the flesh.

The sick bay supplies were very limited, being held for the use of hospitalized cases. So, for any ache or pain, you would receive a small quantity of aspirin powder. A vitamin B-complex powder was brought in, as beriberi became critical. I had a slight case. However, I was able to bite my tongue while the Japanese doctor prodded with a needle, and I came out on the list to receive the full treatment (a daily dose for one month).

Christmas, 1942, found us all at work, but we returned in the evening to find that the dockyard authorities had supplied each man with a polished, red apple. Much to our surprise, everything closed down for five days at the New Year, 1943, which enabled everyone to rest his weary hide, and thaw out.

Ten days after this rest, the first of our contingent died. Reg Malkin was a fine, talented, man of music. Before the war, he worked with his father, an organ maker, and had figured in social and dance band leadership, in Edinburgh. He was a good friend to many of us, and soon became a frustrating and stubborn patient in the sick bay. He literally starved himself to death; he would not eat, and refused to keep clothes on his body, or to remain in bed. Each evening I visited him, I found his ribs protruding a little more, with his sickly smile revealing his teeth, a little whiter.

When we returned from work one evening, we heard of his passing. He had a plain, pinewood coffin, with four other, sick POW's for pallbearers, then a trip across the bay into Nagasaki, to a small Christian church. After cremation, the priests promised to place the ashes under the altar until the end of the war.

At least we all knew what the outcome would be if we succumbed.

During the first three months in Japan, our numbers were reduced quite rapidly. We lost one of our great friends on February 12, 1943, a Canadian known to us as Candy. A very capable man, he was always willing to do what he could for anybody, and for the cause. He succumbed to pneumonia, due to lack of drugs, along with several other fine, well-built fellows. This was a great tragedy for all that knew him. Along with the lack of drugs, the Japanese pressured our doctors to keep all possible men at work, exposing these men to the gale force winds and freezing temperatures.

The interpreter told us this was the coldest winter recorded in forty years, for the southern region of Japan. The large frames of young men were in need of nourishing foods, to supply sufficient energy for a nine-hour day in a dockyard. We received a diet practically free of protein. Soybeans, supplied to round out the daily ration of rice, were the main source, plus supplies of small, sun-dried fish, or squid from time to time. Seaweed was also introduced, which became a major part of many evening meals.

Bath nights had finally been organized, for personnel from a certain number of rooms, each Tuesday and Thursday nights. This meant a brisk walk down to the village public baths, which were comprised of two large baths, built like shallow swimming pools. Each person was permitted three small, wooden bowls of water; the first was used to dampen oneself and lather the soap over the body, and the other two, for rinsing off. This completed, we could then step into the bath, sit down, and soak. The civilian families—men, their wives and children used bath number one, and the POWs used number two. Following the bath nights, there was much discussion at the dockyard between the Japanese, their topic being the size of a white man's penis. From that day on, whenever a man tried to take a leak behind the block piles under the boats, there would always be two or three pairs of eyes, male and/or female, peeking. This was the outcome of communal bathing.

Outside of our visit to the public bath, every week to ten days, we did not wash. I was made more conscious of my dirty underwear, damp with sweat and nauseating odour, and had no possible way of getting them washed and dried. This mode of Japanese cleanliness gave us something in common; we started to scratch like little monkeys, whether we were at work or in the camp. After supper, it became quite customary to remove these inner garments, gradually running a finger under the folds of the seams, giving chase to lice. Catching and cracking them between our thumbnails, and staining them with our own blood, gave a measure of relief, until the next batch hatched and started to feed.

As spring progressed into summer, we encountered another dilemma—fleas. These would actually take flesh as they bit, leaving a row of bumps under any area where the clothing rested fairly tight to the body. While the penis of one man was swollen because of beriberi, another man would be swollen from fleabites. The itching was so bad that one seemed to lose control; the scratching causing open wounds that made a trip to the sick bay necessary, for iodine treatment. Throughout the flea cycle, everybody would awake at least once a night, to try to eliminate a number of fleas. The cracking of their tough hides rang out when they were compressed between thumbnails. When I draped my blanket over the legs of an upturned stool, resting on the table, I saw fleas jump as far as thirty-six inches to evade capture. When I had finally caught and killed one, I placed the carcass safely away until the following morning, so that I could measure the ghastly thing. Up to this day, I still wonder if the leg measurement of three-eighth inches was correct; but they were enormous!

The cold rice we were eating, carried in our lunch boxes, was now causing much stomach trouble. Its acidity, our inability to digest it, plus the fact that it was green, made chewing it properly very difficult. Diarrhea became a problem for many, so small bread buns were brought in daily from a Nagasaki baker, as a substitute, which helped settle most of the troubled men's stomachs.

On our way to the benjo (toilet house), it was necessary to pass a guard box, high above the ground. Ninety percent of the time, this post was not illuminated, but regardless, one had to stop and salute what might be a guard, or an empty box. During the days of the stomach troubles, many men, in their haste for a booth, would try to slip past without making a salute. Consequently, all hell broke loose as the guard set out after the offender. Not only would he catch him, but he would also find the benjo half full of smoke. With additional help, the guards would round up everybody within the building, and have them fall in at attention in front of the guard house—punished, guilty or not.

Failing to salute, one usually returned to his room with a swollen face. The ignored guard meted out corporal punishment, using the face as a punching bag, as he stood on his platform, with the guilty one standing a few steps lower. Finally, to quell smoking in the benjo, smoking privileges were curtailed in the camp for two weeks. It was a godsend to reach the congested areas beneath the boats, to smoke and wile away the hours, constantly on the alert to disperse if any suspicious characters appeared, such as naval guards, gestapo or civilian foremen. If you were working beneath the boats and stood idle, in view of the guards and police around the dry-docks above, you would invariably receive a nut, bolt, or rivet on your head, or some other part of your anatomy.

On two or three occasions during our stay in Fukuoka 2, they were generous enough to supply a quantity of tuna, whale meat, or dried, sockeye salmon cutlets. We understood the salmon had been caught and dried off the West Coast of Canada, and had been stowed for many years, in burlap sacks. This fact we could not discredit, because a third of each cutlet was missing, due to maggot holes. However, what was left, we soon devoured; each man closed his eyes and partook of his morsel until it was gone, none daring to take a peek at what might be in the centre.

One evening, on arrival back at the compound, we were told that too many of us were sick. This could not continue, or there would be nobody left to return to his loved ones after Japan had won the war. Each mouthful of rice should be masticated at least forty times, to ensure proper digestion. This had been proven by the dockyard manager himself, who told of being a victim of tuberculosis, but instead of despairing, he took off, up the side of a mountain. He built a shack, made a garden, and lived in solitude until he returned to his doctor, feeling healed and receiving a clean bill of health. From that day on, he had persevered with his endeavors at the dockyard, and remained free of tuberculosis. Thus, he proved that his advice was the right course to follow.

The routine had become monotonous: the constant working, sleeping and adhering to command, the same old jargon, a smoke or a game of cards if there were no chores.

# 23

---

## *Torpedoed*

As the weather warmed up, we were compelled to wear rubber-soled canvas shoes, styled after the English plimsoll except that the big toe had its own compartment. This was done to preserve our leather boots for the next winter. By now, my boots had been soaking wet for so long that I doubted if they would ever dry out and hold together. These canvas substitutes created a problem if wet, especially when crossing areas adjacent to power cables used for drills and welder's torches. The cables were so poor that the electricity escaped into the ship's decking, giving one a hefty jolt.

A birthday had arrived for one of the Scottish boys. Like the rest of us, he wanted to stay in camp for this day, but unlike us, he went about it the hard way. He deliberately hit his large toenail with a sledgehammer. Sure enough, he hobbled so badly that the guards assigned two fellows to help him back to camp. Naturally, Jock was kidded by those close to him that he would spend his birthday in camp. Well, the Dutch army doctor considered his position, in relation to Japanese commands that all possible men must work, and assigned two, burly medical orderlies to sit down on Jock, after lifting him onto a table. The rest was quite simple. The doctor merely passed a scalpel under the damaged toenail, wrenching it off, while Jock helplessly screamed his head off, using a barrage of obscene threats. A little gauze was dipped in a mild solution of permanganate of potash, applied to the toe, and held with adhesive tape. Poor old Jock was back on the camp work roster the following morning, and with a smaller ration of rice. That was his birthday in camp!

When the reclaimed land area (between the window of our room and the water) became sufficiently large, Japanese carpenters built a new, two-storey barracks block, a steam-heating plant, and bathhouse. The Japanese had hoped to put many more POWs into this addition. Instead, only fifty men arrived of which the majority were Australians, and the balance, Americans. Apparently, the few Americans were from the small Pacific Island of Guam. They arrived there before the war, to complete sentences they had started serving in Alcatraz Penitentiary, in San Francisco, California.

I had met most of the Australians, at one time or another, back in Changi barracks. The members of this small contingent were the only survivors of their battalion, which had been taken to work on the Burma railroad. From the day they arrived at the railhead, friend had to bury friend. None knew who would be next, which comrade you might bury tomorrow, or if that one might be you. Cholera hit so suddenly and severely that no one stood a chance. Burials averaged six or seven per day. This was the toll in one very small sector of the line; it will probably never be known how many were lost on this project.

They told us of submarine action, and about a boatload of prisoners sinking. Among these was the doctor, Squadron Leader Dawson, who had attended my ulcers back at Semplak. The torpedo had struck the ship, splitting her wide open and expelling many prisoners into the water. This fine doctor, a gallant swimmer, saved seven men from drowning by dragging them to a lifeboat before the sharks struck. His death was, I believe, a tremendous loss to the R.A.F. He was a true leader, very capable and well respected by all that worked with him.

The sinking was a typical result when seafaring on the China Sea, and the reason for not using the new barracks building. It was never inhabited, except by these few fortunate survivors. The Japanese excuse was that the building was unsafe! It was of post and beam construction, using mortise and tenon joints, and braced and bracketed. This was far superior to any two-storey, framed building that I have seen erected on the North American continent, since I took up residence here in late 1948. These old tradesmen were masters in tool technique and material application, both in construction within earthquake zones, and in wooden boat building.

Now the new bathhouse was completed, bath rotation came around a little quicker, once a week. Here it was revealed that more and more men were being beaten; black and blue buttocks were displayed. The navy Sergeant was delivering punishment at the dockyard, using a pickaxe handle. The reasons were seldom known! The colour of the skin was so dark and angry looking that you wondered if it would ever be white again.

Work became harder as the demand for shipping increased. We only received one day off from the yard each month. This day was not for resting, but for camp cleaning. We hung blankets in the sun, to get rid of the fleas (and their eggs), and if we were lucky, the chores finished by 3:30 or 4 p.m. Then, adding to the pressure of weariness, two or three might be caught smoking. The orderly NCO would then discipline the whole camp, and there were no further smoking periods that day. To increase output, management singled out those they considered were working well, and gave them extra slices of bread. The additional influx of civilians and young students to the dockyard increased the opportunities for scrounging; thus, little was achieved by the bribes.

At this time, the Japanese had received their first major setbacks in the southern fighting zones. The Americans had won a sea battle, which caused much concern in Japan. The news came from secret sources (out of the English printed paper, the Moinichi Times, which was handed out quite frequently until late 1944), until the bugle boy turned traitor, and revealed the source. This bounced back, to the detriment of our Washington State friend. He was placed on hard labour—carrying pipes and installing them in the bilges of tankers under construction, a minimum of a given footage per day. Fatigue overcame this man, and he died a few months later.

After several requests had been made to the camp commander, permission was finally granted to use the bathhouse as a church, on those Sundays when we were not at the dockyard. Several years before, many of us (regardless of denomination) had tried to explain to our respective vicars our experiences of when and how we had first accepted Christ into our daily lives, and which ultimately led us to be confirmed into the church. But, after many months of the trials and tribulations of POW life, I felt that only within that improvised church were we humble men, doubtful at heart of the immediate future.

We were led into prayer by an officer, and pledged ourselves to God's keeping, asking for His guidance and strength. Only then did any of us realize the true meaning of accepting Christ into our lives; only then did we realize that God is the Light of the World. He gives man the strength needed to survive the perils of living, and only then did we realize His presence as we tried to sing, with a lump in our throats, "We love the place, O God, wherein thine honour dwells; the joy of thine abode all earthly joy excels." Only then did we truly accept Him. It was such an uplift, which gave us the courage to endure, the morale to carry on, and above all, the determination to live. And so, forever should we sing, "O Lord, our God, arise, scatter our enemies and make them fall, confound their politics, frustrate their knavish tricks, and sing with heart and voice, God save us all."

The heavy rains began to fall. It was our second such season since arriving at the camp. During this period, in our first year we were kept in camp on many days, or proceeded to work after the worst part of a storm had passed. Can you imagine trying to run toward something that you have no desire to see? Coolie straw hats and coats had been provided; such provisions meant that our presence at the dockyard was assured. For countless days our feet and legs were soaking wet, no matter how hard one tried to avoid the puddles and flooded dry-docks. Yet, in spite of these conditions, it was surprising how many kept going. At this time of year, a much greater emphasis on the use of the scrubbing brush was stressed. Everyone scrubbed their body a little harder, trying to drive away the goose pimples.

Compressed air played a major role in this yard. Riveters' guns, braziers, and caulking guns depended on it. Maximum output was the call of the day. Consequently, unless a major blackout occurred or the odd transformer blew up, production flowed right along. Competition had suddenly become the dream of management, and hull bottoms were completely plated, ready for riveting. Several teams of Japanese, Dutch and Javanese riveters were allocated, respectively, to number one dock and number two dock. Somehow, these plans had to be stopped, or at least slowed down; by the end of that day, the hose-menders had repaired more hoses than was ever thought possible. Many rivets were also cold-set, because of dwindling heat. With so many concerned about these two units, we were free to relax around the others.

Once again, we managed to put a "tilt" into a forward bulkhead, and we'd accomplished much more work around it before it was noticed. This time, I was part of the crew trying to put the thing right. With a heavy jack and small lengths of poles, the impossible task of lifting began. The short, wood members, which failed to withstand the pressure and split quite readily, caused much concern and created stressful moments. The foreman searched for, and found, a large piece, which he placed on the jack between metal plates. We pulled and struggled with the handle, hoping to elevate the hull plate upward, to the bilge. Although a true position was never achieved, it was close to being correct. With blocks pushed in to hold it, we started to retire for a breather, when suddenly the block exploded out, striking me on the left shin.

I was bowled over into the slimy, thick sludge on the floor, and found it was impossible to stand. I could not put any weight onto my left foot. My friend, Slim, helped me to hobble approximately one-quarter mile to the sick bay. I was in an awful mess; by this time, my leg was double its normal size. The doctor had to put a tight bandage on, to ease pressure. There was one hour to wait before leaving for camp. Slim, and a fellow named Frisby, gave me support under my shoulders, and helped me to shuffle along.

After supper, which I found difficult to hold down, I reported to sick call. The doctor put me on the list to stay in camp the following day. The next morning brought a big change; too many were listed to stay in. We were all examined, and fifty percent of us were returned to the work list. I have no idea how I was able to make it to the dockyard, report for duty, and stay close to the job. The foreman kept me free from duty until early afternoon, when I could no longer stand.

He told Slim to take me to sick bay, and so it was the same ritual of waiting until we would parade back to camp. This time, instead of just assisting me, the boys took turns carrying me piggyback. The following morning, the senior Dutch doctor chose four, huge, Dutch bakers (three hundred pounds each) to hold me down while he plunged his scalpel deep into my shin, releasing a huge abscess. The incision felt as though it was scraped out, and then it was packed with one-inch finger gauze. Cleansing and packing was done every day for three weeks, while I stayed in bed. I was then given light duties in camp.

# 24

—

## *A Woman's Chores & Raw Cement*

The jobs in camp were limited mainly to garden work, and were often harder than in the dockyard, as you were constantly under the surveillance of one or more guards. It was during these camp chores that I witnessed three Japanese women at work. Tied up to the campground, in close proximity to the lats (latrines), stood a huge, covered, wooden barge. It was usual for the operators of these types of vessels to live, and raise their families, within quarters built at one end of the barge or boat. The unit was supplied by the government, and it became his lifetime career. There was no engine, and the operator propelled it with a long oar at the rear. As it was all done manually, he must have been thankful when there was good weather. In this particular case, the man was old, and the helpers were his wife and two daughters. His job was completed when they tied up, and then the women started to work.

They placed a flimsy plank from the barge deck, or roof (which was level with the gunwale), to form a gangplank. Then, they proceeded to the lats and opened two manholes in the floor, to gain access to the tank (50 feet x 3 feet x 6 feet deep). The stench was terrible, so bad they tied scarves around their head and mouth, as a gas mask. They started bailing it out, carrying the sewage in two small barrels dangling by ropes attached to a pole. These were then emptied into the tanks of the barge. Using this method, these women were kept busy for days at a time.

When, how, or who cooked the food on the barge, was a good question. I also wondered what might happen if, in a storm (with the old man struggling, out on top), the bulkhead between the tanks and living quarters was to start leaking, or give way. As to why they should want to take the sewage, gardeners need plenty of fertilizer, to enable them to produce all those little oranges you love to eat at Christmas time. (Do you? I don't!)

In another phase of work, the women were used as gleaners, working in pairs. One would sweep and shovel the waste that accumulated in the bilge of the boats and around the ships' extremities. Her partner would haul it away, with her little pole and baskets, to large mats. These were hoisted by cranes, and dumped into large piles at one end of the dock. Another group of women would sit all day, at one of these piles, extracting all the metal, such as bolts, nuts, washers, reamer drillings, electric welding rods, etc., for smelting down. When my wound had healed sufficiently and I returned to the dockyard, I found myself (with a few other buddies) at such a pile.

After two weeks, I was ready for the insane asylum, and requested to be moved. I considered a caulking job, and was transferred to caulk within one of the new dry-docks, working under and up the sides of a boat, like a little ant. I fired a small, chisel-shaped tool with a small air hammer, as I went, trying to seal the seam of the plates together. This was fine until, one evening, the POW caulkers were held back to caulk up an engine room. The English sailors had riveted it, with semi-cold rivets.

We found the water test was on, and all the rivets were leaking, like a colander. We grasped the message; work until it is tight. I applied the tool to the rivet's edge, and pressed the trigger. The rivet swiveled, and water squirted over my face. After cutting several notches, I finally got enough metal to roll over, and squeezed it tight. Wedged seams where three plates meet were impossible to caulk.

Hemp packing was also applied but failed to stop the leaks. There were several other places like these and they were finally welded. This was the hardest four hours that I ever worked within the dockyard. Just how much of the Pacific's turbulence it survived, we will never know. The POW's were raced back to camp and on route ten American aircraft were seen heading north. They suddenly changed course with a 90° turn to the right and dropped their bombs. Two columns of smoke appeared in the east, the other side of the peninsula. It wasn't until after the war that we found out what the targets were.

During 1943, production from the dock installation did not progress as fast as the Japanese had anticipated. Consequently, many of us were transferred to the cement mixing and pouring operations, or the rock-crushing machine. A huge pile of rock always stood alongside a platform, which housed the crusher. For many days, the men would each pick up a rock and walk along the ramp, then drop it into the machine and pass on down the other side. This was then repeated. The idea of forming a human chain, and passing the rocks along, never crossed their simple minds.

The foreman had previously worked in a British Columbia lumber camp, where he was in charge of the operation, and he would shout, "Speedo, speedo." The more he shouted, the slower the movement became. Regardless of his efforts to try to increase the volume of rock to the ramp, he never did gain more than two or three pieces ahead of the machine's capacity. During his frustration, he slapped faces. He'd spit in your face, and jab his little stick between your ribs. These small abuses tested our morale, and self control, almost beyond endurance, and yet, the incidents were accepted and passed off by all of us. This was another example of their ignorance, not dealing with us as intelligent and civilized men, but more often, like pigs.

Those not detailed for crushing operations were deployed to shovel pebbles, or mixed sand and gravel, to feed the mixer. Another dozen or so men were used to move, open, and feed cement into the mixer. The rest of the men were high up on flimsy scaffolding, bound together with straw rope. The boards, over which they dragged and pushed carts of ready-mix, were thin. Each one bent so much that ruts formed, which made it difficult to keep the carts rolling. Nobody dared stand close beneath these structures because boards did break, causing the cart to tip and fall off, almost pulling the operators with it.

We worked in pairs; one pulled on a rope attached to the front of the cart, while the one behind lifted the handles and did the steering. My partner, Sid, and I had a bad experience; the cart went over with the broken board, and I was left sitting with my legs through the hole. Meanwhile, the rope, which Sid had luckily placed over his shoulder, pulled him over backwards and left him lying flat on his back. If, like some of the others, he had placed the rope around his waist, Sid would have gone down with the cart.

At various times throughout each day, water, cement, or both were absent from the loads being tipped into the forms, making it a difficult task for the men staged at intervals around the forms. Using small wooden hammers (mallets), they tapped the forms, to vibrate the cement into a tight-settling position. With a lack of water in the mix, no indication was given of the built-up level since there was no seepage between the seams of the forms. To alleviate this, a request would be passed along to the mixers for a watery mix to follow. When this mix arrived, the tipping had to be adjusted according to its absorption into the dryer material, otherwise, it could result in a deluge of water seeping through the forms, soaking the tappers.

My job became most unbearable, especially for the fellows held to a fixed position among the scaffolds and forms, where the only movement was the swing of an arm. So, the opportunity to slip something over on them was always seized. The old civilian had to descend for his smoke, so we would then ascend with only half the mixture. Two days later, after two pillars plus a crossbeam had been poured, the civvies arrived ahead of us, to remove the forms. They were late on this morning, so the guards and gestapo held us, in line, while the forms were being removed. But, after a few sections had been moved from the base of each pillar, the workman called a halt. Then, after a short consultation with the guards, we were dismissed to proceed with our work.

The civvies were livid with rage. As they had started to remove the forms, they had detected enough raw (unmixed) materials, that if they exposed the pillars in front of the gestapo, they would have been put away for a long time. Gradually, a lower form was eased off, and the pebble, gravel and sand, all began to fall out. It was hard to gauge how much; it was anybody's guess. However, the fallout ceased and the form was replaced. We were trying to look busy, biting our tongues so that a smile would not break out. Overhead, a second group removed a couple of sections, to enable a galvanized chute to be inserted. Then, with the first batch of mix ready, pouring commenced, filling the cavities first. Simultaneously, four other civvies checked out the high beam; about fifteen percent was lost. Finally, a check of the second pillar revealed a cavity that was approximately one cubic yard, so a half-day was lost in patch-up work.

For our work in the dockyards, which I understood were controlled by Mitsubishi (others claim Kawaminami), each man was paid ten cents a day. It was never received in cash, but was signed for, then spent by the camp store's accountant. This supplied five cigarettes a day, plus a few cookies or oranges, when they were available. These were normally delivered to the camp on a Friday.

I was returned to caulking, a job that usually gave one a blackened face. Warmth brought with it a concession to wash our hands in the courtyard tubs, but not the face. The first evening, the sergeant caught eight of us wiping our faces with the damp towel. Immediately, we were put on six weeks of fatigues, starting upon arrival back in camp each day.

Our chore was to build a garden; this made donkeys out of us. The camp was built on rock, with a gravel surface. This meant only one thing; we had to transfer soil from beneath the cliff bluff, at the entrance to the camp, into an area marked out by a day crew. Armed with a pole with two baskets attached, I started out on the coolie jog, for two hours. That bastard caught many others during our first two weeks of fatigues. He assigned them to clean out an area adjacent to the roadway, which ran some twenty feet above camp level. It was here that another day crew was given the task of building an air raid shelter.

# 25

---

## *Tragedy*

**1943** was a year in which the Japanese workers gave all they had towards building ships. The yard completed thirteen boats, and it was indicated that 1944 would be an even better year. In addition to the docks already in production, the new dock would hold two units, one on each side of the caisson (the dividing gate, installed at the centre of this huge dock).

The first of two boats being built had gone ahead with great speed. It was now in the outer half of the new dock, complete and ready for sea trials. A full complement of crew and naval personnel were on board. Guns were mounted, stores stowed, steam was up, but there she stood on the blocks, waiting for the most essential thing… water!

Meanwhile, in the inner half of the dock, a keel with its bowsprit section, stern-post and rear bulkheads, was now in position. The hull's bottom plates were in place, and the platers, ship carpenters, and riveters were all striving to keep up, so they would not delay the lowering of bilge plate sections by crane crews. At the sea gate, crews worked around the clock to get the last loads of rock moved away and to pour the vital gate section, which would enable the completed boat to reach the sea.

Some unforeseen trouble was encountered at the northeast corner of the dock, and a full week passed with the boat still waiting to exit. Progress in the inner half had now advanced to a finished bottom shell (complete with bilges) and two more bulkheads, with some side plates positioned.

It was a morning of fruition, with a bright sunny sky, and our assignment was to work on the hull plates, in the inside half of the dock. We arrived late and were without incentive to enter the dock and disappear into the black, damp, dismal surroundings beneath a sheet of steel. The riveters and their crews would waste an hour or so gathering up their guns, braziers, and air hoses. Other caulkers, like myself, required the services of a blacksmith, to reshape and harden (temper) the caulking tools. This meant we had to visit a building about four hundred yards from the dock.

Army, navy, and gestapo guards all checked us out, and became equally mad when each of us produced five tools, none with serviceable heads. They could not harden the steel, and consequently, the power of the gun caused it to burr, or snap the end off, as it made contact with the plates. This delay was our salvation! While we were in the blacksmith's shop, the final charge of dynamite had been detonated. It cut too deeply, and the incoming sea lifted the gate and rampaged into the dock, carrying everything before it. The completed boat was lifted from the blocks and thrust through the caisson, its mast heads catching the overhead cranes as it went. Simultaneously, as the water swirled in beneath, the shell was also lifted and pushed, by the plunging boat, halfway out of the dock, with the forecastle coming to rest across the main, dockyard road. Disaster had struck; alarms sounded everywhere, and guards, on the double, rushed around in circles to round up the POWs. This was the first, outward sign given that there was concern for our welfare, as workers on a military target. Immediately, we were dispatched to the campgrounds, in units of approximately fifty, where we awaited the final count. It revealed that not one POW had been lost. A miracle had saved us, but it was an unanswered mystery to the bosses who had detailed so many to work on this unit.

Four days were spent in camp while the mess was cleared away. As far as we could see, nothing had been salvaged. The speed of the water was estimated at 80 mph, and the unofficial disclosure of the number of lost Japanese, by their fellow workers, was ninety dead. Some claimed as many as a hundred and twenty. They swarmed over these projects like ants, so the higher figure could not be discounted. Only God knows where the cranes landed; there were three to each dock.

By midsummer of 1944, our lives had become stereotyped and monotonous. I believe we all waited for each evening to close in, when we would crawl into bed after roll call, and shut everybody out, to meditate. This was our only privacy in which to think of our loved ones at home, say a prayer of thanks to God for bringing us safely through another day, and request His guidance and protection throughout the next. Then, we could drop off into oblivion, away from it all, until the abrupt awakening for a visit to the lats. A guard's fist punching your head, demanding you get up and straighten your wooden slippers, which were kicked out of position by a buddy making his way to the lats. Or, another fool is caught smoking in the lats, so all the camp must stand to attention for hours on end.

They maintained a theory that if twenty men took ten hours to complete a job, forty men would complete it in five hours, or eighty men, in two and half hours. In most cases, where the numbers were increased for speedier results, we found the lack of space did not permit us to function properly. The more crowded we were, the easier it was to delay the operation, causing more frustration than results for those responsible.

From this time on, we noted the civilians were losing morale; setbacks from both the front lines and the home front were cutting into their optimism. More and more of their ranks were missing from morning roll call, being thinned out by extensive drafts into the armed services. The replacements were young students, who we noticed had been drilled in school, strictly for future combat and military careers. The aggressiveness shown by many of these boys towards the POWs caused consternation and arguments between themselves and the old, Japanese veterans. Where we would try and keep the older man free from trouble, we would antagonize and thwart every movement of the youngster. By the end of 1944, we could see our own achievements.

Like students in any other country, they realized the necessity of boosting morale within their own ranks. Large billboards were erected on the square in Boys Town, to the advantage of all who passed to or from the dockyard. Each day as we returned to camp, the latest bulletins from the front were posted, in the form of captioned pictures. Terrific claims were being made against the United States Navy, with descriptive scenes of sinking aircraft carriers, battleships, destroyers, and submarines. Colossal figures were marked up against the airforce bomber and fighter commands.

We were receiving good news through the Moinichi Times. Tidbits, smuggled to us from an interpreter, told of Americans advancing from Guadalcanal, the Gilbert and Solomon Islands. Through this medium, we had heard of these battles without many frills attached, so our reactions to the billboards were not pessimistic as they had expected. Instead, we were pleased, and it caused many of us to smile. The guards became quite hostile, handing out many hard hits, on unprotected rib cages, with their rifle butts.

Upon arrival in camp, we were put into the usual formation (lined up before an elevated platform) to await a speech from the Commandant. First, he listened to an account of our reaction to the posters, then he turned to address us with a question. "Why is it that after so many months of you being POWs, we of the Nippon Army have failed to break your morale?" Many of us bore severe bruises from corporal punishment, but there was only one answer, "We shall be taken from here shortly, to help in the defeat of the Germans." Naturally, we were all quite aware that our physical condition was far beyond any such dream. However, it was an excellent way of keeping ourselves sane; the idea had good intentions.

Arriving home (at camp), our first thoughts were on the up-coming meal, seeking the possible issue of some wee morsel from the Red Cross parcels. Although it was stated that a parcel, per man, had been shipped each month, the estimated receipt averaged one parcel, per year, for each man. That evening, after the meeting with the Commandant, a four-ounce can of butter, between three men, became a part of our meal. There was no occasion when picking from these parcels would give a man his unchallenged share. It became increasingly difficult to share out these small cans between odd numbers. At no time could lots be drawn, or men divided according to a percentage some receiving today, with the balance to receive the next issue. Already, far too many were in debt from the loaning or borrowing of rice rations, so it made one unwilling to accept a gamble on a few goodies that were made available.

For several months, we in room 20 chose to close our eyes to the fact that five fellows had teamed up with a few from room 19, to raid the Japanese cookhouse. They stole close to a bucket of rice, and would snack, around 1:00 to 2:00 a.m., each night. The inevitable happened, and at about 1:30 a.m., the rice-raiders were finally seen leaving the cookhouse. A guard, making an unscheduled visit down one of the corridors, had not been detected, and saw movement in the part of the barracks that was out of bounds between the sounding of lights out, and reveille. Instantly, the whole camp was brought to its feet; everyone was brought to the attention for a long, long stand before being released for breakfast, then on to work. It felt a tremendous relief to get lost in the complex of the dockyard. We all realized the incident was far from over, so to be out of sight was to be out of mind, for the time being.

Upon returning to camp, we were regrouped, into room formation. From this, many rooms were quickly eliminated, leaving three, which were always more penalized than the others. These were rooms 19, 20, and 21. Room nineteen was comprised of all American boys, room twenty was half American and half English, and room twenty-one was English and Irish. So, for the exploits of eight men, we others were held too, waiting for the responsible parties to reveal their identities. We had lost three and a half hours sleep the night before, and now a further two hours, after a day's work. But, with a pail of rice between eight for so many days, they must have deemed it was all worthwhile. Possibly, but only until after the rest of us had been dismissed.

Then, the guards went to work. Each of the eight, in turn, received the full treatment of jujitsu throws and chops, from each of the guards in attendance, starting with the Sergeant Major who was of Mongolian extract. He was a fine-looking specimen of a man, with full, broad shoulders. He really gave a good display of how to throw a person. Each POW received his share of bruises, and felt aches and pains for weeks after. Later, they were crammed into three boxes (known as the slammer), each with a floor area of two feet by two feet, and stayed there for two weeks. They were built so that it was impossible for them to sit down. When the American Major complained of the conditions, he was put in with them; a man of six and a half feet, made it a tight fit.

We fellows kept our word of agreement (made many moons back), and each of the five from room 20 still drew their ration of food. Each day, one by one, they would take their chance and break from a camp work party, or detour from benjo call (latrines), to devour, like ravenous wolves, the servings that were hidden in their kit. These rations were a direct donation from the room's food box. The other members each made a donation, because we were five rations less in our quota.

# 26

---

## *Our American Roommates*

An unusual treat was dished up for supper; each man was to receive a boiled potato. Room 20's box was two potatoes short. A fellow from our room, a cook, had taken them out while en route from the kitchen. He confessed to the act, and promised to attend confessions on Friday. But one fellow spoke out, "You bloody fool! How does that replace the potatoes?"

Incidentally, this fellow occupied the space next to me, and a couple of weeks later he gave me a rude awakening. His stomach was giving him a lot of pain, which gave me a trip to the doctor's mess for assistance. The diagnosis was appendicitis. Removal to the hospital was impossible at that early hour, and after receiving a good dose of aspirin, he sweated it out until after we had left for the dock. What was remarkable, however, was the Japanese doctor claimed it was the largest appendix he had ever seen.

One of the American boys, known only as Corky, had an enormous body frame and muscles equal to any Hercules. It was difficult to try to make conversation, because he had never attended school and could not read or write. Corky was brought up on a ranch where he had been taught to manhandle and brand steers. To identify himself he would say, "My name is Corky. I live on the King Ranch, the largest ranch in Texas." His strength excelled over anything I had ever seen.

Their group came from many different parts of the U.S.A. As I recall: Minchew (Carolina), White (Texas), Gilmore (Alabama), Martin (Chicago), and Sergeants Scott and Robinson (California). There was Donahue, who lost a number of phalanges from his toes, having been frost bitten. Another three, Pollock, Drake, and Hughes were also from the southern states. Then, there were the Valdez brothers, who were quite good guitar players from Mexico.

Our relationship was very good, with a fair amount of give and take. How they loved to gamble! Anything that came to the room for distribution (and it was never enough to go around), they wanted shared by drawing your number from a hat. I was in dire need of some additional warmth for my legs. The draw for one pair of super, wool long johns proved good to me; I won them!

Cimex lectularius (bedbugs) are blood-sucking, evil-smelling insects. They became almost unbearable during the summer of 1944. Most of us would rise in the morning with huge wheals on our necks, the size of fifty-cent pieces. They were painful and aggravating. Efforts were made to dispose of the bedbugs with steam from the cookhouse exhaust. A cleaning crew would take all of our belongings away from both sides of a wall, to access their hiding places. It worked to a degree, but they were back again before it could be repeated. Each wall took a day to clean. A serious problem arose throughout the whole camp, concerning several of the boys. Regulations did not permit fellows to associate from one room to another. But through trading, it did happen, and a rice bankruptcy claim was submitted to our officers. One fellow owed as many as thirty-nine half bowls of rice, which he had accepted as payment for doing dhobi (laundry) for his mates. The crunch was inevitable because we did not receive a day off each week, plus he had also borrowed from one in order to pay another, putting himself deeper in the mire. To protect these fellows, and ensure they would eat a full meal, all dealings were cancelled.

Toward the end of May 1945 and with Okinawa in American hands, the Japanese made up three train loads of POWs and moved them north of Nagasaki. It appeared they were making last ditch efforts to defend the homeland. With the Americans working toward an invasion, the balance of us (around four hundred) would be easier to evacuate. Rumors were being told that it would be total annihilation of all POWs if the Americans did invade.

Having observed the effectiveness of the gong, we started up many false alarms, shouting "Storky!" In turn, the young students would plunge for the hammer, to sound the alarm. Each time, a mass exodus to the caves followed. What a disruption of plans it created! Then, big raids started, in late July 1945.

# 27

—

## *We are Not Forgotten*

"Americano! Americano!" the young students shouted as they ran in terror to the air raid shelters. We followed at a slower pace. The guards were irritable; it was the third such episode that day, July 28, 1945.

We entered a cliff-cave, one of four or five areas that had been blasted out. The rock was used for land reclamation, extending the new dry-dock installations which were continuously advancing out into the sea. Sitting just inside the entrance, I had a commanding view. Thousands were scrambling in every direction to their designated shelters. Simultaneously, planes appeared. They did not turn to attack us as expected, but continued on their northward course. There were three or four fighter-types, including twin-fuselage Lightnings, escorting B-29 Bombers. From our hole in the cliff, we were able to count one hundred and sixty-nine. What a sight, as the sun glistened on the sleek, aluminum objects!

Minutes later, thunderous explosions echoed toward us. Jubilant shouts went up, much to the disapproval of the guards, but they also knew their position was becoming hopeless. For months now, Japanese fighters had failed to show over Nagasaki. This was a shot in the arm for us. We were all geared up, in high spirits almost to the point of becoming defiant. "They are about to receive a taste of their own medicine! Soon, we can take revenge for the treatment we've received." Each man had an account to settle with one or more of the guards, whether they were soldier, kigoon, or gestapo.

It seemed as though we had sat there a long time before the "all clear" sounded. We found ourselves being hustled back to work. No sooner had we reached the centre of the road, where we were fully exposed, when there suddenly appeared from behind us, over the rock bluff, ten Grumman Hellcat fighters, just fifty feet above our heads.

We were flabbergasted! Immediately, caps were thrown into the air as we waved wildly. The guards were stunned. For the first time in three and a half years, we saw friends coming to our aid; we had not been deserted. Tears blurred my vision and I was choked with emotion. The pilots acknowledged us by dipping their wings, and then jettisoned their auxiliary gas tanks as they flew on over Nagasaki harbour. No doubt, they were from one of the aircraft carriers steaming offshore. We all darted back into the cave for a further delay from work.

We wondered why there was no counterattack or anti-aircraft fire. The aircraft carriers must be quite close for their planes to be playing hide-and-seek. By the time we finally returned to our work stations, it was time to stow away our tools, fall in, and march back to camp, about two miles south. We were moving on air, wanting to call out and chat with our comrades. It was difficult to maintain a steady marching pace in our excitement.

The guards were showing signs of animosity toward us; they had become nervous seeing the enemy so close at hand for the first time. If they caught one of us with a smirk or grin on his face, it was quickly slapped off, or a rifle butt put to our ribs. Some were pulled from the ranks, made to touch their toes and then struck a blow on the buttocks with a pickaxe handle. Tension remained even after returning to our rooms. Over our bowls of rice and seaweed soup, we refrained from jubilant speech or any other display of pleasure.

Over the next three days, we saw similar displays of air power. Since the beginning of the air raids, the number of guards had been increased when we marched to and from camp. Many were young boys carrying wooden rifles, the only "weapon" they would receive. They derived great pleasure using them to dig us in the ribs. A lot of trouble might have developed had we not felt the war was just about finished. For a couple of days, heavy clouds rolled over, curtailing activity in the air.

At five in the morning, the strains of the bugler's "Ta ta, ta ta, ta ta ta" broke the silence. We commenced the day with our usual body scrub. As dawn broke and the sun pierced through scattered clouds, we could see renewed joy in the faces of our comrades. Anticipation of further allied action gave us courage to get out and endure another day. It was August 9, 1945, and we didn't feel we could survive another winter.

Conforming to the monotonous, daily routine, we were herded out to the parade ground. Each room was cleared in sequence. A mandatory count was taken, and we were off, marching toward the dockyard. We appeared a bedraggled lot; due to our loss of weight, our clothing hung loosely over skeletal frames. My five-foot, eight-inch frame was reduced to eighty-four pounds. Only sheer optimism and hope that we would eventually return home kept me going.

The road from the camp rose steeply, leveling out beneath a small plateau where an ack-ack battery was stationed. Here, they manned five or six anti-aircraft guns, the main defence for the dockyard area. The sky, brighter now with larger patches of blue, gave the boys hope of further air strikes. To hear some say, "When I get home…", instead of, "If I get home…", was music to me. Now, we were assuring ourselves that going home shortly was a real possibility. To the east beyond a placid sea, a high mountain covered in conifers was cast in silhouette by the rising sun. From the road which was now descending toward the dockyard, we could see Nagasaki, approximately three or four miles to the north.

There were still some clouds in the sky. A mumbling from the boys ahead grew into audible sentences. "Did you see that? There it is again! I'm sure there is a plane in the clouds over Nagasaki!" If this were true, it would be the earliest air attack we'd yet experienced and would confirm our belief that operations against Japan were being stepped up.

Before we reached Boys Town and the naval barracks, it was confirmed beyond doubt that a plane was in the vicinity. We came to a halt before the barracks, and counting of POWs by the kigoons took place. All were accounted for, and we were handed over to the dockyard gestapo for dispersal to our respective sections of the yard. It was about 7:30 a.m.

Immediately, the sirens started. At the double, we went to the shelters. However, the alarm was short-lived and everyone made their way back into the yard. I was now working in the new dry-dock which was capable of holding a ship the size of the *Queen Mary*. Due to an urgent need for supply vessels, the size of boats now being built had been considerably reduced, allowing them to be built much faster. Also, smaller boats made difficult targets, and increased chances of getting through the blockades.

I was caulking the stern of a small tanker which stood in the northeast corner of this huge dry-dock. Looking between the pillars of concrete rising above me, holding four or five floors of maintenance shops, I could see the blue sky over Nagasaki. It was within this view that I clearly saw a plane circling, unchallenged, over the city which was out of my sight.

I was one of four POWs, working with a young student and a civilian foreman, who was also our interpreter. The foreman had come back to work that morning. He had just returned from Hiroshima where he had found his home and family destroyed by the bomb dropped on August 6th. He was numbed, and still in shock. Work had no significance for him, nor us, as we idled away the morning.

At approximately 10:50 a.m. by the foreman's watch, the students drew our attention to a distant object visible within the limits of our patch of blue sky. It appeared to be suspended on parachutes. Moments later, a blinding white flash, brighter than a thousand rising suns, engulfed us.

# 28

## *The A-bomb*

Following the flash, I did not hear any loud bang. In fact, there was a period of total silence, broken only by the clanging of the gong. Between the steps and me was some nine hundred feet, with several obstacles: piles of debris, poles, keel blocks, and scrap metal strewn everywhere. Our group started to move out, every man for himself, in fear that the caisson would collapse and the sea rush in and swallow us up. I looked upward and saw the five stories of flimsy walls, which were built between the concrete, gradually bulge and burst open. The whole side of the installation appeared like a vast honeycomb.

Loose articles, set in motion by the blast, were floating out above us and crashed in our pathway. I became breathless and terribly hot, as if I had just opened an oven door. My movement was curtailed; I was in a vacuum, exerting myself to the limit, but to no avail. Suddenly, the pressure released me and I fell headlong towards the floor, then staggered on. As I made progress toward safety, the articles from above were now raining down, bouncing and cascading around us as we attempted to get clear. There were some resounding crescendos as the boat and floor were hit. A desk and swivel chair landed too close for comfort, just as I made the steps, and I ascended, beneath the steel protective cover over the steps, to ground level.

At this point, I was exhausted with fear, but panic urged me toward the hole in the cliff. By the time I reached the road, pandemonium had broken loose. Thousands, who came from the city, were in a quandary as to what they should do; the boats could not take them home. Everybody was headed for the ferry dock, en masse, creating total congestion on the roadway. The students from Boys Town, the Koreans (men and women), plus the POWs had to pass through this area in order to exit the yard and get to our respective quarters. There was crushing and trampling as everyone tried to clear the area, in fear of being trapped in a direct attack.

The guards directed us into small groups as soon as we appeared, and forced a passage through the mob. We headed directly to the camp and into the shelters. To our astonishment, we saw that the rear side of the camp building had been compressed in by the blast. It had ricochetted off the side of the mountain that was immediately behind the camp, approximately two miles from where we were scrounging.

Gradually, we eased our way out to watch the mushroom-shaped formation of dirt and gases churn its way skyward over Nagasaki, then roll outward to hang over the city like an opened umbrella. A slight breeze was evident, but this did not deter the massive shape from forming. (It's hard to recall how long it took for it to disperse, but I believe it was between two and three days.) The boys said, "Two bombers are making a reconnaissance of the area," as we watched planes fly around the perimeter. Outspoken discussion erupted, and the general consensus was that it was a new type of bomb.

We had finally witnessed retaliation after being on the receiving end for three and half years. It was some measure of reprisal for the vast number of our friends who had died from starvation and physical abuse. Now, there was no doubt in our minds that the end of the war was close. We had never seen more than ten Japanese fighter-planes during our stay of two years and nine months at Fukuoka #2. We were taken back to the yard on the following morning, to dig holes adjacent to the working areas. However, this was quickly abandoned, and we made an immediate departure for camp.

As we headed back, we met many casualties from Nagasaki. Normally, the ferries would have disembarked many workers for the dockyard, but today it was a cargo without a future. These people had been burned, and in fact many were charred on areas that were exposed to the elements prior to the detonation of the bomb. Medically, it appeared little could be done for most of them, quickly enough.

During the course of conversation, we surmised that it was possible for this type of burn to have automatically cauterized itself, and that the patient could manage until their turn came for a clean up. In many cases, the charcoal had dropped off, leaving areas of exposed bone, and it was isolated to one or more of the limbs, mainly arms. We considered, in this case, the chance of survival was very good. Others, who were injured on the torso itself, would have a tremendous fight to make a good recovery.

As we discussed these people, we did not know of the damaging effects of radiation. This was something new, since we had left England, and not included in the manuals on defence and self-preservation in warfare. When we learned of these problems and considered those with damaged torsos, we realized that little could be done. The victims showed no pain, and eventually slipped away into oblivion.

I have often thought of Tubby, who sat with us with his piece of chalk, discussing the war's progress. Could it be that he still lives with that moment, as I do? And just what are his views on it today? I remember well discussing such a bomb, and its magnitude, when at the flight training school, and recall the desires of the designer to make its effect equal to that of an earthquake. It became a reality, and was put to extremely good use: opening up tunnels, dropping viaducts, and destroying many other vital targets such as the U-boat docks. The bombs were tail-fused, and penetrated twenty-five feet of concrete, surprising the submarine-builders beneath.

Forty-eight hours after our return to camp, we each received a bottle of light lager, brewed in Tokyo. It was refreshing. We kept a low profile for the next few days. Overnight, our guards left and the Dutch took over the camp security. On August 15, 1945, Emperor Hirohito announced the Japanese surrender in a radio broadcast. (The formal surrender to General Douglas MacArthur took place on the quarterdeck of the battleship *U.S.S. Missouri (Mighty Mo)* in Tokyo Bay, on September 2, 1945.) Three Squadron boys left camp to head for Tokyo, where they had hoped to join the Allied Forces for a quick trip home. This was impossible, as communications between the main islands had ceased to operate, and they returned to camp with the bad news.

While they were north of Nagasaki and with POWs from a camp of American crewmen, they learned of an atrocity that had taken place. A group of young Japanese officers took American airmen (the figure of seventy stays with me), and using their swords, jabbed, cut, sliced, and slowly dissected each one. Each airman was compelled to stand and watch, awaiting his turn and wondering if he was next. This was a human blood bath, which to this day few know about, and many never will. Were these officers ever brought to trial? For me, this remains one of the unanswered questions of World War II.

# 29

---

## *Brought Out to Freedom Through Ocean Perils*

From the day of the Japanese surrender, we formed groups and set out to satisfy our curiosity about what was behind the rock bluff. This was on the other side of the road, which passed the camp and was used by the male Koreans on their way to the dockyard. Around a large bend, we came to the entrance of a coal mine; the miners walked in, down a gradient, to the coal face, which was now deserted.

Heading north, we found a large school, which stood overlooking the sea. Here we discovered the answer to the black column of smoke seen after the American bombers had passed, sometime ago. They had hit the two vessels that had been launched from the dockyard and were doing some sea trials. The boats had sunk in shallow water, leaving their superstructure exposed, and were temporarily out of service.

The men of our room became involved in a sports day, competing against the other rooms. I coached a tug-of-war team, and we finished in second place. We were so good that we even took one pull against the Dutch bakers, who averaged three hundred pounds each compared to our meagre eighty-four pounds. The day was well into the afternoon when a squadron of B-29s came over, dropping us supplies. They had welded three steel drums together, and these were dropped on parachutes. There was very little warning, and several of the boys had to dive out of the way to avoid being hit.

The drop was scattered out, almost to the dockyard, and we did a lot of carrying to retrieve it. The contents were exciting; there was much needed, prepackaged meals (providing three meals per day), plus clothing, socks, and boots. One set of drums had split open on impact; the velocity pushed the soap in the first drum into the toothpaste in the second, and both were crushed into the chocolate in the third. We arrived to see small children scooping the jumbled mess into their mouths. We then became good Samaritans, diverting the children with handouts of the same three commodities, but some which were still intact. They went home full of excitement. We didn't know how upset their little tummies were since they were already distended from malnutrition.

It was August 31, 1945, my brother's birthday. The Dutch claimed it a day of celebration for Queen Wilhelmina's birthday. The rice that was cooked for the evening meal was the last from the kitchen, and we took advantage of the pre-packed meals, according to the label. It was wise to follow the instructions given as they prevented gorging.

On September 11, 1945, which was my wife's birthday, units of the American 11th Fleet sailed into Nagasaki harbour. During the evening, the Admiral visited the camp, taking a list of particulars, and made an announcement, "We shall take you out as soon as we have a decontamination centre built." We could not give praise or rejoice enough.

Two patients, very sick with tuberculosis (who had come from the *H.M.S. Exeter*), were taken out immediately. We later heard they arrived and met their wives, only to succumb a few hours later.

To our amazement, first thing Thursday morning, September 13, 1945 (my sister Ruth's birthday), landing transports arrived and took us to the Nagasaki quayside. They brought us past the dockyard, located on the north side of the entrance, into the harbour. The installation was all steel, and we saw a tangled, twisted mass of girders that had melted with the heat from the bomb. It was a vast contrast to the concrete superstructure where we worked. We landed right behind the American Red Cross ship, which I believe was named *Hope*.

The seamen had installed a number of large cubicles, complete with showers and hot running water from the ship. The small bags we carried were doused with DDT powder. Then, we discarded our clothes into a container, destined for the incinerator. We passed from cubicle to cubicle, lathering and scrubbing ourselves from head to toe each time, as we passed along. An orderly, with a large magnifying glass, scoured us to ensure we were cleansed. We received some shorts, a shirt and slippers, and could choose either a New Testament or Rosary. Welcomed by the priest, we entered a tender and were put on board the *U.S.S. Chenanago*, an escort carrier (or "baby flat top").

All planes had been dispersed, and the top hanger was covered with cots complete with bedding. This was total luxury, with delicious meals and a super deck of three-inch steel (to combat Kamikaze attacks), where we could walk. Sunday morning was even more gratifying, with the Padre conducting a full service on deck, complete with the band and a full parade of all ranks. The music was great, and with everybody singing, made it all very sacred and hallowed.

A few days later, we slipped quietly out of the bay, to the open sea and headed due south towards Okinawa. A destroyer escort was about two miles ahead of us, and after a couple of pleasant, sunny days, the sea started to roughen. I was standing near the stern on the starboard side, listening to a young sailor speaking of home, when a rusty looking object appeared, displaying several spikes. We realized it was a mine. The sailor grabbed a flare, threw it out to mark the spot, and telegraphed the bridge.

With the water's flow, it gradually came closer, and my friend gave an order to lie flat against the superstructure, away from the rails. Luckily, the wash from the propellers kept the mine clear of the stern post. The Captain signaled the destroyer, which turned back and traced the mine. It took six shots to blow it up. A huge volume of water was created, like a waterspout. If the mine had struck us, we would have sunk, as the stern post is one of the most vulnerable points of a ship.

The following day, we came into a man-made, floating harbour (similar to the Mulberry Harbours used in Normandy), and landed on Okinawa. Just when the *Chenanago* had stopped, the landing was recalled and we hastily pulled out to sea. There were approximately three thousand ships around the island, assembled for the invasion of Japan. A total withdrawal was made, and we all headed out into the path of a typhoon. Once again, I experienced a savage sea, which rocked and rolled us about for two and a half days. We reached the eye of the storm, where the ocean was completely calm for a few hours. Then, we encountered a sea of greater turbulence, and winds of one hundred and eighty miles per hour. During the fourth night, it was at its worst, with the POWs lying on their cots, sleep an impossibility.

At the same time, the crew (wearing their life jackets), were ready to jump overboard. Apparently, the boat with its added three inches of steel deck was now top-heavy. This reduced the maximum list, which was only seventeen degrees, at which it would capsize. That night, the boat did just that, twice! We lay there like innocent ducks. It's hard to believe that in the short time since our release from the POW camp, our lives were almost taken at sea. We landed and walked into a tent camp; everything had been wiped out. The surrounding area was battle-scared, with several concrete slabs where Japanese soldiers had died. Many chose death in preference to surrender.

One of the many boats returned, and dropped its landing ramp onto the beach. It brought three huge refrigerators full of Coca-Cola, which were dragged up to the camp. These were opened twice a day, and for refreshment, the men (in single-file) were permitted to take a bottle, and drink it within the area. Bottles were not allowed to be carried away. A second one was served, provided it would be drunk and not wasted; it was a free issue. The Americans fed us well, and provided good entertainment, a cinema show with vivid scenes of the Pacific campaign. There were some large and costly battles, total carnage everywhere.

A new adventure awaited us very early on the third morning. Nine Liberator bombers took seven POWs each, and we left Okinawa for Clarke Field on the island of Luzon, in the Philippines. We flew in formation, and I sat in a gunner's position (the port side, fuselage blister), which was complete with gun installed. This experience gave me an insight of the importance of this position in defence of the plane. This part of the world was well known for its air turbulence, and the wing showed great resilience. This was a necessity when carrying eight-thousand plus pounds of bombs, and four engines, otherwise, they would have snapped off.

Clarke field was huge, with a very long runway lined on both sides with thousands of planes of different types, as far as the eye could see. These were ready for the invasion of Japan. It was beyond one's imagination to visualize them in operation, or the devastation they could create. We were transferred immediately onto a Douglas DC-3 aircraft (used heavily in troop transportation) for continuation of our journey to the capital, Manila, being used as a receiving station for us POW expatriates.

After take off, a change of weather forecast was received by the pilot. He made a dash onto Manila's airfield. In fact, the descent was so steep we almost plummeted to earth. It was a great three-point landing, just as the aerodrome became socked-in with a deluge of water. Some planes were compelled to divert to other landing strips and were held over for three days. Meanwhile, we who made it received a wonderful reception. We went to a compound that handled British personnel, where the M3 division (English secret service) received each man individually. Complete reports were made on all aspects of our internment, and included those who we considered were guilty of war crimes. Medical checks were made, and much-needed clothing (of Australian origin) was also issued. Finally, we were able to cablegram news of our well-being and the arrangements regarding our embarkation for home.

# 30

## *Guest of the British Fleet to Vancouver, BC, Canada*

On my birthday, September 25, 1945, we were put onto Britain's queen of the fleet, the aircraft carrier *H.M.S. Implacable*. The number one hangar was set up with bunk beds, where we were received by a full complement of nurses (Scottish) and put into bed. We were confined until a further medical check was made, which was done as we sailed from the Philippines. The diagnosis was made; we all required one week of a solid protein diet. However, we were free to walk and enjoy the cruise. We watched the huge wake, which looked like a four-lane highway at the stern, made by four screws (propellors). We were sailing towards Honolulu, Hawaii, at a good speed, and passed Wake Island, which was off the port side.

Sailing into open water, there were no more islands until we reached Hawaii. The weather was good to us, but time was not kind, it lingered on. The Captain gave us an unexpected display one night. He opened up all his weapons for a sparkling show, like fireworks. There was so much, it appeared impossible that any aircraft could penetrate and make an effective attack.

When we crossed the date line, the calendar stood still; we lived the same day twice. It became cloudy and miserable, with reduced visibility and white-capped waves. At times during our daily walk on the deck, we even became wrapped in cloud. We were now back on a balanced diet, which was a big relief. The all-protein diet was a hard thing to take. However, I certainly felt like a different man, easy in movement and with energy to burn. We were all mustered on the deck as we entered Pearl Harbour. Just prior to everybody being brought to the attention, Slim and I were fortunate to have our names drawn from a hat for a trip into Honolulu.

We each withdrew eleven dollars for our trip, and rode a liberty bus. Enroute, we passed through vast fields of pineapple, and saw a large water tower, shaped like a pineapple, with the large inscription, "Del Monte". Our stay in Honolulu was limited to three hours, and as we strolled down one street full of restaurants, we felt hungry. We made quite a hit with our Australian clothing, complete with the famous hat. We entered a steak house just as two sailors were being served steak and chips. They took one look at their plates and felt unable to stomach it, so the proprietor offered them to us. It was a scrumptious meal, on the house.

Thousands of sailors were roaming everywhere; many of them overloaded with beer. We visited a couple of souvenir stores, then it was time to find a ride back to Pearl Harbour. Several buses were available, but it was a scramble to get on board. Arriving back at the docks, the guards and military police were extremely busy. The bus stopped in the centre of numerous wire pens, and many sailors were being hauled into them for having been in town without a pass, in other words AWOL. Before Slim and I went back to the *H.M.S. Implacable,* we made a detour to the quayside where the *Arizona* was sunk. We paid tribute to all those lost to the Japanese bombing, with a few moments of silent prayer. Our buddies were interested in what we had seen, and in a number of photographs we had bought. Time was too short to browse around town and see all its landmarks, or to visit the famous Waikiki Beach, just too far away.

Early the following morning, we were already out to sea and heading for Vancouver, British Columbia, Canada. *H.M.S. Implacable*, often referred to as the "Sleek Lady", was met by thousands of small boats and yachts in the Strait of Georgia, and a plane from the *Vancouver Sun* newspaper was overhead. At 10 a.m. on October 11, 1945, we arrived, under patches of fog, and glided under the Lions Gate Bridge with inches to spare, into the CPR docks. Thousands of people welcomed us home; many hoping to receive news of loved ones who were not with us. Reporters from the *Vancouver Sun* newspaper collected stories. The throngs were so thick it was almost impossible to move; some of my Canadian relatives were out there somewhere, but could not reach the station platform to meet me. The Canadian Pacific Railway took four trains of army personnel to eastern Canada, on the southern route.

The R.A.F. boys took leave of our senior officer alongside the ship. We filed over to the Canadian National train, which would take us by the northern route to Truro, Nova Scotia. Our trip took us first to Blue River; the trees in the full colours of fall, with mountain peaks looming up on almost every curve. It was magnificent scenery all the way, not forgetting the mighty Fraser River as we traveled through the canyon. We spent an hour in Jasper, Alberta, where Slim and I received the last bottle of beer. Our first big stop and celebrations were in Edmonton. The ladies catered to us from several tables loaded with tons of goodies. Then, on to Saskatoon, Saskatchewan, for more of the same, and the contrasting scenery of the prairies.

It was two in the morning when we pulled into Winnipeg, Manitoba. Many families were out seeking their loved ones from the Hong Kong campaign. It was from here that the Winnipeg Rifles were sent overseas, with many of the boys from local communities. Sgt. Rice, one of the 242 Squadron, lived here and left us to visit his family, joining us later for England. He had married a Welsh lady during the time we were stationed in North Wales.

The CN coach had excellent accommodations, and the cooks catered good meals all the way to Truro. Buses took us ten miles north, to Debert camp and the R.C.A.F. base. First thing the following morning, we were outfitted properly with R.A.F. clothing, which included a group of ladies who stitched on our stripes and medal strips.

It was at breakfast where we were introduced to maple syrup. The Mess Sergeant was peddling a beautiful, baby doll. Two or three days later, after much discussion and cajoling, I purchased it for what I considered a fair price. In all the years as a POW I had only received two letters from my wife, Marjorie, which told me a daughter had been born to my older sister. Knowing this gave me the incentive to buy the doll. On our first Sunday in Debert, two hundred and seventy-five cars came and took us for what seemed a long drive through Nova Scotia. We were split into two groups, and the half I was with went to Pictou, where a branch of the Canadian Legion gave us a good reception. It was a small, boat building community, with a nice looking hull on the stocks. Good yarns were told, as good ale was downed. We met a lot of hunters returning home, with their prize deer on car racks. Our host gave a number, of so-many points, on the antlers of the large ones; he said that it was an indication of the buck's age. Does were not included in the hunt.

Behind the barrack block, beyond the fence, stood the Aero Cafe, and it was usually our last port of call for the day. After a supper of beans on toast, and playing a song called "I don't want to be Aladdin" on the jukebox, we would crawl through the fence, and to bed. At one-thirty a.m. a fire engine left the aerodrome, speeding to a fire, and in the distance we saw what were obviously whole buildings engulfed in flames. On a frosty morning, after breakfast, Slim and I walked about a mile in the rising sun. The concrete footings were all that remained; even the plates had burnt right out. Later, we heard that some fifty head of cattle had been lost.

We spent about eighteen days at Debert camp before embarkation orders arrived. It was a seventy-mile train ride to Halifax, to board the French liner *Ile de France* (51,000 tons). I was given a beautiful berth in an "A" deck cabin. I volunteered to work in the ship's orderly room, and checked out the passenger list for a count of those on board. The lower decks had been completely stripped of all cabins, leaving vast areas of steel decks where bunks, built six high, had been installed. As a troop ship, she transported in excess of 12,000 troops per sailing. The only part of the ship's peacetime furnishings not changed, was the chapel. Very rich in gilt and velvet trimmings, with cushioned seats on mahogany pews, its beauty left me speechless, with complete solitude and contentment.

Sailing time from Halifax to Southhampton was three and one half days on a very placid Atlantic, total serenity in itself. Fog was prevalent in The Solent as we approached Southampton, and several tugboats nudged us into the quayside. Engines stopped throbbing, the hawsers were attached, and we were safely back in England at last. It was November 8, 1945, and approximately four years had passed since I said good-bye to my wife.

Just before 11 a.m. I was called, over the inter-com, to report to the officer in charge of the gangplank. He handed me a fifteen-minute pass, to go ashore where Marjorie was waiting. When we met, she was not sure that I was Bill. "You have changed!" was her comment, with a brief embrace. I was embarrassed, and could not reply. I finally expressed my feelings, that I was grateful to be back home, and realized that after four years apart with no communication, we were total strangers. It was difficult to convey to my buddies just how awful an experience it was. Mine was not a case of falling into each other's arms, because I was the unknown quantity, and after all that time, and not by choice, we had lost touch. The outcome was, of course, "love heals".

# 31

—

## *Dispersal Centre*

The R.A.F. section disembarked and we boarded a train to take us to a large depot (#10 R.R.G. Personnel Dispersal Centre) in Wolverhampton. Just south of Oxford, the train passed my home within two hundred yards. During the years I was away, the two-line track had become part of a twelve-line marshalling yard. This had completely taken over my friend's dairy farm.

We entered the mess hall at 7 p.m. to find a small banquet had been laid out for us, with a wonderful group of R.A.F. and W.A.F. personnel supplying all the services. It was so gratifying, but we were overcome with emotion. We had tears in our eyes, lumps in our throats; it was hard to accept the compassion shown towards us after receiving so much abuse. Gradually, we settled down with a glass of wine (some preferred beer) to enjoy a bountiful dinner, prepared by a chef who did an excellent job.

The next several days involved a number of important procedures, the priority being our interrogation by a large number of officers from the government MI9 department. Everybody, in turn, gave their own personal account of POW days. We covered the location and term served in each camp, treatment, punishment, working conditions, marches, and food. This was necessary to determine the degree of atrocities, and possible trial of the offenders under a war crimes tribunal.

The medical board was great. They covered our complete anatomy for any complications due to malnutrition, or diseases such as TB. Eye, ear, nose, and throat specialists, also dentists, left nothing to be desired. Injuries were dealt with by a special panel, following medical assessment. A general consensus was attained and given in the following announcement: "You have lost fifty percent of your life expectancy", and it was recommended we immediately refrain from smoking, and drinking liquor.

The final interview covered rehabilitation, with many of us receiving offers to stay with the Royal Air Force. Several did because they had lived in below standard conditions before the war, including poverty. An alternative was given to those wishing to learn a trade of their choosing, at one of several trade schools across the country. At the time of mobilization, the company boss had orders from government to hold a man's job for up to three months after his release. Because of this, it was mandatory for one like myself to return to that job.

I did pursue the possibilities of a business on my own, cabinet making, only to discover the severe rationing of materials, and high prices. There were jobs available in that industry, but with very low salaries, which convinced me to return to the Alden Press. Those who were confined to the Sick Bay remained for treatment. The rest of us received a pass for Christmas leave, to return by January 6, 1946. Following a pay parade, I sent a telegram home, giving the time of my train arrival in Oxford, at 8 p.m. It was a dark night and a fast journey as we flashed past groups of lights, which signified stations and towns, stopping only at principal cities.

Marjorie and Dad met me in the sombre light of the platform. This time there seemed to be a measure of warmth and comfort as they said, "Welcome home." For a few moments I was choked up, and found it difficult to respond. To crown it all, Mr. Hearne and his taxi were waiting, the same cab and driver who took me on that one-way trip to the station in 1939.

My brother, Leonard, had left a few days earlier to report back to the Royal Marines. He had received his papers and was conscripted for two year's service. Prior to his leaving, he had assembled an illuminated welcome home sign over the front door. Underneath stood my mother and our next door neighbour, Mrs. Spencer. Then the tears began to roll. Once we had sat down and composed ourselves, the conversation flowed eloquently. Over a cup of tea and a plate of hot, "Welsh Rabbit" (Welsh rarebit), I felt a sense of security returning.

During 1943, Marjorie had seized the opportunity to buy a three-year old house. It was a rare commodity, found on the market at a time when building was at a standstill, and thousands of homes were being destroyed in the air raids. It was located just four miles from home, with a good bus service. We hopped onto the last bus of the day to arrive at a smart looking, semi-detached three-bedroom house, furnished with pieces as they were released by the Wartime Measures Act. It was cozy, and we settled in for the night, not to sleep, just discussing immediate issues at hand, such as occupation, expenses, the pros and cons of budgeting, and how much longer Marjorie would remain at the University Press. But, the major question was, would my salary support such a choice property?

I drifted away into a deep sleep, only to wake up with the pounding of the front door knocker. The baker, with his basket of hot bread, lured me, standing in pajamas, to open the door. I chose from loaves of Hovis brown, Youma malt, French, raisin, and regular pan bread. I slipped on a pair of trousers and stepped out, to take my first peek at what we would make home. I became ecstatic; before me was a very long garden, with a small orchard at the bottom. My father had also been in to help Marjorie with lawns, a strawberry patch, and a vegetable garden. And still, I could see a great potential with future additions.

Christmas hit me hard. The rich festivities were beyond my capabilities to handle, and as much as I wished to eat a good turkey dinner, I just couldn't do it. The plate was placed before me and I picked up a knife and fork. After three or four mouthfuls my stomach refused it. I broke out in a cold sweat, and felt as if the end of the world had come. I was forced to vacate the dining room and go out into the cool evening air. At New Year's we had a special engagement at a dance (I never did dance). The same type of sensations prevailed, and compelled me to retire once again. I felt so depressed, that the day I returned to base it seemed as though civvy street was not for me. A final interview determined my status; I was placed on "A" release, for a further recall to duty if required.

The clothing store gradually brought me out of my crisis as I chose from the vast aisles of clothes. I came away with a very good wardrobe, complete with outer garments. The tailors ensured I was well fitted; I felt good and was handsomely dressed.

January 9, 1946, I left Hennesford for the last time, complete with my packed uniform, leave passes, food ration book, and release papers, which included a return rail pass, if ever needed. Final payments would be forwarded by cheque. When they arrived, enclosed was a further request for me to stay with the R.A.F., with promotion. My response was, "I really did have my bellyful", and stayed free.

# 32

—

## *Rehabilitation & Emigration*

I returned to the Alden Press a happy man, with the determination to make a good home and participate in local community affairs. Within the confines of the factory, with the noise from the printing presses and dust from the various papers I was handling, I became a victim of claustrophobia. After spending the past six and a half years out in the open spaces, confinement was not for me.

Marjorie answered a local advertisement, which resulted in our purchasing a greengrocer's shop. We took possession on July 1, 1946. This gave me many hours outside, preparing and stocking vegetables, during which time Marjorie handled the inside groceries. A year later on July 19, 1947, our first child arrived, a beautiful daughter, Rosalind Judith. In reply to a request I had made to the Royal Marines, my brother was given leave to assist with our chores, until he could join us permanently.

We enjoyed a great relationship with our customers, since they were all previous neighbours of ours, but I could not purchase enough in volume to do justice to their loyalty. Considering this to be a major problem, I appealed to the Ministry of Food, which was still rationing all commodities. The statement we received was, "Your quotas are based upon previous, pre-war sales, and until quantities produced are increased, we cannot grant your request."

The store was located across the road, opposite the city soccer ground. Most Saturdays a game would be played, by either the First or Second Division teams. The spectators would buy fruit to munch on during the game. Most other items, such as chocolate bars, were rationed and required a number of points from their ration book to make a purchase. Apples were the main item, and invariably 8–40 lb. boxes sold during a three-hour period. Everyone came in to give us a boost; their way of saying thank you for our past war services. Marjorie had nursed with the Red Cross during her spare time from the Oxford University Press. She had given many hours of assistance to thousands of army personnel who survived the beaches of Dunkirk. Their injuries required a lot of attention, and they had arrived at the Radcliffe Infirmary, Oxford, by the trainload.

In mid 1948, an extremely good offer was made for our business. I recalled the days when I visited the Kensington Museums and the films they showed of the British Empire. On many occasions, I became very intrigued by what was said of Canada. I had built up a desire to become a part of it, and now, I visualized, the dream could come true. Canada looked to Europe for tradesmen after the war, and others who could assist with the large farms. Striking pictures of the prairies, golden with grain, proclaimed, "The breadbasket of the world." Also, they listed the many manufacturing plants, "A land of plenty, with all the new materials they need."

We considered, finally, that here was the very place where a young family can grow and prosper. Canada House accepted us after the necessary forms and medical requirements had been completed, not forgetting that the required funds to be self-supporting for a minimum of three months had to be guaranteed. We accepted the offer (we could not refuse), and added the money from the sale of the house. We three, and my brother Leonard, made our exodus. Our parents gave us their blessings. We had visions they might join us one day, but later they declined our offers.

We flew on the North Star plane, Trans Canada Airlines. Due to inclement weather, a diversion was made. Leonard was holding his cup of coffee as we were eating dinner over Scotland. We dropped into an air pocket, which left his cup hanging on the ceiling, as we journeyed to Reykjavik, Iceland. Continuation into Canada was also on a changed route, from Labrador down into Dorval Airport, in Montreal. It took three attempts to land as the aerodrome was socked in by fog. On the first two attempts, we saw the floodlit runway, as if it were night, and each time we almost hit the watchtower. With a vicious climb, almost vertical, the pilot saved us, and we went back up, into beautiful sunlight. With a third circling of the airport, we came down, hitting the runway with a tremendous thud. I have often thought that was one landing we should not have made; the risks were too high.

This was our first point of arrival in Canada, and where our passports were endorsed, "Landed immigrant, Dorval Airport, PQ, October 26, 1948". Two hours later, we flew on to Toronto, where we were met by one of our former customers, who was on a visit. After a long wait, we made a second hop into Winnipeg, then at 3 a.m. on to Lethbridge, Alberta, and then finally, to Vancouver. That morning we ate breakfast over the Rockies; it was the most beautiful view of the snow-capped mountains I have ever seen. The trip from door to door took twenty-eight hours.

We spent a week in Vancouver with our great-aunt, who had missed me at the docks on my way home from Japan. We sailed for Victoria on the ship, *Princess Victoria*, which pitched and rolled all the way. It was impossible to dine as the turbulence and winds of 90 mph made it difficult to move. The weight of the crockery in the cupboards burst the doors open, and it crashed, in smithereens, on the dining room floor. The lounge seats slid to-and-fro, from the sides of the boat towards the centre walls. Rosalind (15 months old) was thrown from Marjorie's lap, and Len dived forward, grabbing her before she hit the bulkhead.

How the ship missed hitting the rocks on either side of Active Pass, one will never know. The Captain headed into the harbour, although many thought we would ride out the storm in Juan de Fuca Strait. Cousin Leslie, an excellent shipwright with the CPR., later told Leonard that on our trip the boat did hit, and dented a plate. Auntie Mabel, with cousin Marjorie, met us; they were shivering cold, standing with little to no shelter against the force of the storm. It was a day to remember, Wednesday, November 3, 1948. We had arrived in Victoria, British Columbia.

Rehabilitation was not easy, as work was in a degree of recession due to approaching winter. What a winter! My uncle claimed, "Victoria has not seen snow like this since the heavy snows of 1916, when the army was called out to assist with the "clearing." The first three winters we experienced were extremely cold, with snowfalls that kept us on the sidelines. Leonard was able to gain a good position, and became an expert in linoleum and carpet laying. I took three or four diversified jobs before entering the softwood lumber industry in 1953, for the second time.

First, I learnt of the various species of trees that put British Columbia in the forefront of world markets. Douglas Fir was the most sought after in the field of construction, because of its strength-to-weight ratios and its fine texture in finishing products. White Fir, Western Hemlock, Western Red Cedar, White Spruce, along with Idaho White, Ponderosa, and Lodgepole Pines, all found a place within the merchantable lumber markets. They were all manufactured into products for both interior and exterior use. For well over a hundred years, Douglas Fir was supplied for railroad ties and material for rolling stock, which were used extensively throughout the British Isles.

The British Admiralty, too, bought ship's plank and deck materials along with mast and spar stock, from the day they first sailed into BC waters. These items were over and above all the timber bought for domestic uses in Canada, and around the world. It became obvious to me that this was a lucrative and demanding industry of which I should become a part.

I had previously worked for eighteen months in a sawmill factory where I was taught how to identify some lumber species. These were termed "patterned stock", under the "Uppers classification", which I assembled into window and door frames. From this work, I visualized the complexities involved in lumber grading, which occurs after the breaking down of a log into various groups. Ahead of me lay a long and arduous time of study. "The art of lumber grading" is a great challenge, to correctly apply the grade to a piece of sawn or planed lumber. No two pieces are alike, and several years of practical experience are needed before one can assess, on one turning of the piece, all the irregularities allowed within a grade. When a chain is moving the lumber in front of you at six hundred feet a minute, a keen eye is needed, in co-ordination with the mind, to detect irregularities before your crayon can mark, denoting the grade.

Each year, written and practical exams are held for graders to maintain, or improve their certificate. Not until the day I was given the task of standing before some forty students, as a teacher, did I realize how little I knew. However, I was successful, and became an inspector with the Pacific Lumber Inspection Bureau. In 1967, they awarded me the position of supervisor, and I moved to Toronto. I processed claims against shipments of lumber to various points of Eastern Canada, and also to the United States, from Iowa to the Atlantic Seaboard.

All of the problems between the United States and Canadian marketing boards did not, and do not, pertain to the volume of lumber going into the States from Canada (this is classified in the States as dumping). American sawmills became idle because the logs they should have processed were shipped offshore in the round (in their raw state). The Canadian industry did not take jobs away or lay hundreds idle in this manner. All products shipped from Canada first passed through the sawmills.

During my seventeen years in the claims department, I visited many lumber dealerships and prefabricating plants, which were manufacturing homes and trailer units. They did not use West Coast species of Douglas fir and Hemlock, because their jigs and machines were unable to handle the heavier and tougher fibre. Their orders and demands were for Western White Spruce, a species not grown in the States. It is strong, but light in weight, and a spike (nail) could be set by the nailing tool. The species was grown in heavily wooded areas, mixed with Lodgepole Pine and White Fir. It was, and still is, marketed under the grade stamp, as "S.P.F. kiln dried". Here, it should be noted that the drying percentages are ambiguous, and were a bone of contention for all my thirty-three years working within the industry.

Even today, it has created greater problems. "K.D." (kiln dried), is a designation accepted by the American and Canadian lumber standards. They state that "Dry" is 19% (moisture content) or less. "Green" is 20% or more. Some orders could be 15% or less, and stamped "M.C.15". Whatever type of construction is used, or if new materials are applied, this moisture should not be encased within vapour barriers, without a means of escape. The quality of grades has been reduced, and the grade stamp abused. Its purpose was to protect buyers, using supervised graders to denote the grade of the piece to which the stamp is applied. Today, stamping often shows "#2 & Btr." (better). This defeats the purpose and deceives the end user, especially when the grade #2 is permitted areas of decay. As one can see, with the allowable moisture content, decay is automatically activated.

While on one such claim, I was visiting Chicago the day President Richard Nixon opened the new sewage treatment plant, built on the waterfront of Lake Michigan. During the ceremonies, the Chief Engineer responsible for the building of the plant offered Mr. Nixon a glass of pure, clear water, which was declined with some remark which I did not hear. However, the engineer explained that the new plant processes the sewage, and the water is purer than that in your household taps or the lake into which it is being returned. To prove his point, he showed no qualms and drank the refused glass of water himself.

I acted as an ambassador to the United States, for Canada's lumber industry, and built a good relationship between buyers and vendors. Those I met asked me, pleaded with me, to stop the shipment of logs offshore from the United States. That was beyond my jurisdiction, and I suggested they bring it before the Governors of State, also the Senators and Congressmen. Their reply was, "They will not listen." So, this is how vast areas of the Northwest United States, and Washington State including the Olympic Peninsula, became devastated. Where was Green Peace then? During my time in Toronto, I received word that it was almost impossible to enter Port Angeles, due to the enormous booming and piling of logs.

It is interesting to note, that even with the enormous volume of timber shipped or used domestically from BC forests over the years, BC forests and treed parks still cover an area equal to two and one half times that of the British Isles. During all my years in the sawmill, watching ten-foot diameter logs come through the head rig (and some even larger, requiring dynamite to quarter them), I did not encounter a tree older than seven hundred years. So, I would like to know how Green Peace can assess a tree at a thousand years old?

I retired on September 29, 1984, from a very happy span of employment within B.C.'s forest industry.

# Epilogue

I have now passed my eighty-fourth birthday, and it is most distressing to watch everything we strived for disintegrating before us. We, the Veterans, did a great job for Canada and our children, but now it is all being destroyed through world marketing with restrictive measures of production compounded by the North American Free Trade Act. These measures have created so many lost jobs, and drastically reduced wages and consumer buying power. They will not protect our children, but put them out as slaves. Their need for an education will or may not be met because university costs will be far out of reach.

Governments have smitten us, and those responsible were not rubbing shoulders with us during the big struggle. Therefore, they did not get the message, as we did, that to have lost the war, would have been the end of civilization, as we knew it. Trying to save it became the incentive to fight and live.

What bothers me most, is the total lack of unity across the country. Up until the early sixties, we had achieved a thriving economy with an excellent standard of living. Our government bodies have failed to control the exploitation by financial institutions. Interest rates are compounded to the point where annual profits have become absolutely revolting. The word that sums this up is no longer "extortion", but "grand larceny", in my opinion.

There have been occasions in Parliament when the odd voice has been heard broaching the subject of interest, but it has always been suppressed and brushed aside. This brings about a disturbing situation which forces those hurt by the credit/interest problems, to enter the demoralizing standard of "poverty". Meanwhile, the Honorable Members (although I cannot see why they should be addressed as such) choose to give themselves exorbitant pensions.

This wealth must be shared; live and let live. Everybody deserves a place where they can live in happy co-existence. Those responsible for failing to avert conditions of poverty, must come to the aid of those on welfare. The wealthy should realize that they entered the world with nothing, and are certainly going to leave with nothing.

## "You Can't Take it With You!"

When I was back in Oxford, England, in 1999, and speaking with my nephew, I was told the river Thames had reached a point of almost being too clean. Some species of fish can no longer exist in it. There is no such thing as secondary treatment of sewage pouring into the river, as we have here in British Columbia.

In England, all excrement becomes fertilizer, and all other solids are destroyed by incineration. The heat produced is used for steam generators, supplying thousands of kilowatts of electricity to the grid system. All gray water passes through a process of purification and then goes back to the river.

900 million dollars was spent for an addition to the British Columbia lower mainland sewer installations to handle and pump processed sewage out onto the continental shelf, which suffered extensive damage back in the late fifties. If you consider increased population from immigrants and new families, it never will be adequate. Just imagine how many electric toilets 900 million dollars would buy, and the relief on the sewer system they would have made.

It's hard for me to conceive that some seventy years have passed since I was told of the Oxford scientists and their success in splitting the atom. Long overdue is the total development of the "Nuclear Age" which can do so much for mankind, where as proven, man-made contributions are falling farther behind, with astronomical costs. Its heat alone can incinerate all of man's garbage, and generate power so that we can stop building more dams. We could improve sewage systems by the use of electric toilets powered by the nuclear power stations. I believe the harnessing of radiation is just around the corner. Evaporating off the gray water, instead of polluting the rivers and oceans, would give a sturgeon a break.

On May 21, 1955, my brother, Leonard, married Ollie Mair, a daughter of a renowned Victoria, BC, family. They are the proud parents of a daughter Denise, and a son, Eric. Denise and her husband, Jerome Beauchamp, live in Williams Lake, BC, where they have worked as schoolteachers for many years. They are now settled in with two daughters, Tracey and Ashley. Eric, still a bachelor, is thriving with his business as a builder.

Leonard and I have made several trips home to England, the most notable being the celebration with Mum and Dad on their Golden Wedding anniversary, June 12, 1968. With us was Len's family and those of our sisters, Mary and Ruth. My parents have since passed away: Dad in June 1971, and Mum in May 1976.

Mr. and Mrs. Marsland celebrated their Diamond Wedding anniversary on August 9, 1990.

In Victoria, our two sons were born: Ian on October 12, 1949, and David, on May 2, 1953. Marjorie and I never did heal from those four years we were apart during the war. In that time, we were denied correspondence, leaving us totally isolated. Then, from 1953, for thirteen years our marriage suffered due to my work being night shift much of the time. We eventually failed in our efforts to keep our marriage (of almost twenty-five years) intact.

Our daughter Rosalind's marriage to Gary Kobley in 1964, gave us three grandchildren: Deborah Rose, Catherine, and Wayne. She remarried in 1989, to Robert Plumtree, and is now also stepmother to Tony, Jacqueline, and Jessica. They live in Abbotsford, BC, where Robert owns and operates an auto repair shop. Rosalind has been active with the Fraser Valley Symphony since its formation, teaches violin, and does the bookkeeping for Robert's shop.

Our son Ian, an oboist, began his career with the Victoria Symphony. He moved to take a position with the Regina Symphony where he met and married his first wife, Theresa, and had a daughter, Clare. He is presently with Orchestra London, in London, ON, where he has remarried, and lives with his wife, Suzanne.

Our second son David married his wife, Jennifer, in Victoria, and has three children: Erin, Andrew, and

Michael. They have lived in Kelowna for over ten years now, where they have a horse-boarding farm.

It was a terrible blow to everyone when Marjorie suffered for almost two years before she succumbed to Lou Gehrig's disease (ALS) on February 29, 1992.

I have been blessed with five great-grandchildren: Wayne Kobley and Dianna's son, James; Catherine and Nigel Berke's sons, Ryker and Ladnar; and Erin and Trevor Mossop's son, Taylor and daughter, Julia.

More than twenty years have passed since I joined up with my partner, Phyllis. This expanded my family to include her sons, Lance and Darren, and daughters, Linda and Karla, and their families. During that time, I have accomplished many projects in woodwork, with Phyllis and her expertise adding the final, finishing touches. My interests in horticulture have been reduced considerably, partly through health-related problems.

In November 1991, suspicions were raised of possible cancer of the prostate and bladder by Dr. David Froese in Abbotsford. A biopsy was taken in June 1992, followed with a T.V.R. in July of the same year, which confirmed cancer lesions in the bladder, but the prostate tested benign. Several procedures followed, done by Dr. Wayne Cyr of M.S.A. Hospital in Abbotsford, which proved most successful. His expertise and dedication to his patients in this field, has been outstanding. Dr. Cyr kept a constant course of follow-up checks, later finding the prostate was also involved. I received a course of radiation treatments at the Surrey Memorial Hospital, and at this time, I have been declared free of cancer. Additional periodic checks will continue. It's been ten years now, and words can never express my thanks and gratitude to Dr. Wayne Cyr for his untiring efforts for my cause. We live in the eastern part of Aldergrove, BC, now known as the western extremities of Abbotsford, where I hope to be for a little while yet!

Today, as I look back, I still visualize the skylarks and plovers, with their songs and "pee'wits", as they soar high over the fields of golden grain. I stand to watch and listen, holding a freshly picked basket of dandelion heads or elderberries. The sun is bright in a blue sky with small patches of white clouds. Before I reach grandmother's house where she will make my wares into wine, the church bells ring out across the meadows.

That setting was still there last year, and I appreciated it even more so. The only difference was myself, much older and carrying scars of war. A piece of my left shinbone was broken away, and further deterioration occurred through infection, established as osteomyelitis. Later, the problem with varicose veins and thrombo-phlebitis put my leg into a support stocking for the rest of my days.

The blow from the Kigoon, (a Japanese sailor), rifle butt was such that it fractured a rib. It still shows prominently in X-rays today. I was blind from a sliver of steel piercing my right eye, and vision was lost for eighteen months. The Japanese doctor spent many daily attempts before it was finally removed. A cataract formed over the scar, which has been taken off, giving my eye back most of its sight.

The heat of the "A" bomb somehow spared me the torture it could have inflicted, and it is through the power of God's will that I can still move, though slower and with a cane. That scene was so peaceful and serene. As I write, seated in similar surroundings, I reflect on words from my childhood.

If we were naughty, Grandmother always promised us punishment by the "great big fire". We are heading that way fast, unless man changes his policies and attempts to give happiness to all mankind. For the earth will be blown to pieces, and it will return to the sun from whence it came.

# To Those Who Served

How Can We Ever Hope To Know
The suffering you'll never show.
All that pain, still etched so deep,
Forever in your soul you'll keep.
How can we ever comprehend
The wounds that time will never mend.
Tortured souls still search for peace;
For some the hurt will never cease.
How could we help? How can we share
The burdens which you have to bear?
We'll offer prayers to God above,
And pledge to you support and love.
Written by Ann MacDonald of Lime Grove, Southmoor,
Abingdon, who was inspired by listening to Arthur Titherington,
A veteran of the Japanese prison camps, talking on radio recently.

# Nagasaki Memories Still Burn

*by Kurt Langmann*
(from the *Aldergrove Star—August 2, 1995*)

It was fifty years ago this weekend that the final, horrific deathknell ended the war to end all wars. On August 6, 1945, an event fraught with immense implications for the fate of all mankind took place, as an American B-29 bomber dropped a single A-bomb on Hiroshima that packed 2,000 times the power of any bomb ever before used in war. The single blast destroyed 60% of the city, flattening an area of over two miles and killing an estimated 58,000 persons outright and a similar number who subsequently died of wounds, burns and shock.

Two days later, the Soviet Union declared war on Japan and launched an all out offensive in Manchuria, in accordance with the then-secret Allied terms of the Yalta Conference held in February. With the European theatre quiet after Germany's surrender, Japan was crumbling under the onslaught even before all of the Allied forces could be moved into southeast Asia, but still there was no reply from Japanese Emperor Hirohito to demands for unconditional surrender. The next day, August 9, another A-bomb was dropped on Nagasaki and its destruction rivaled the Hiroshima tragedy. On the following day, Japan announced its acceptance of the Potsdam Conference terms, and the war was over. Formal signing by foreign minister Mamoru Shigemitsu was aboard the U.S. battleship *Missouri* in Tokyo Bay, September 2, which is the official V-J (Victory over Japan) Day.

While the Japanese surrender carried the caveat that there would be no "demand which prejudices the prerogatives of His Majesty as a Sovereign Ruler" it was a complete defeat for a man whose megalomania rivalled that of any imperialistic conqueror in history. However, Allied supreme commander General Douglas MacArthur feared chaos and anarchy in the devastated Japanese islands without Hirohito as a defacto "leader" of his people, and spared him the subsequent war crime trials which saw the execution of General Tojo and half a dozen others. While Hirohito voiced the public proclamations, beginning with the renouncement of his "godliness", they were all on orders from MacArthur. In short order, Japan's constitution was reformed to allow universal suffrage and creation of parliamentary democracy, and America largely financed their construction of the country's infrastructure and economy.

The Emperor, who called himself Showa—"man of peace and enlightenment"—passed away peacefully in 1989 and was buried with his favourite microscope and Mickey Mouse watch, in a contentious ceremony attended by most world leaders. The contention arose from the perception by many people both inside and outside of Japan that history was revised, if not perverted, in fashioning Hirohito as a kindly and benevolent gentleman who was manipulated by his militaristic court. There has also been an insistence by some academics and historians that not only was the use of the A-bomb unnecessary to end the war, but that the U.S. government knew that it was not needed.

American history professor Martin Sherwin was recently in Vancouver to speak of the opening of a photographic display of the Nagasaki bombing, showing at Vancouver Library until August 9. Titled "Forbidden Views" in reference to a furious controversy that erupted at the Smithsonian Institute in Washington last year, the photos show horrific scenes of the human tragedy at Nagasaki. Veterans have accused the Smithsonian of rewriting history "to portray the Japanese as nothing but helpless victims and was insulting to veterans of the Pacific campaign," said *Vancouver Sun* reporter Doug Ward in a July 26 article. Ward quoted Sherwin as saying that, "There were other ways of ending the war that the (U.S.) administration was fully aware of." Ward wrote that, "all that was needed to secure the surrender of Japan was an American promise to maintain the throne occupied by Emperor Hirohito…the Truman administration used the examples of Nagasaki and Hiroshima to send a shudder across the world, intimidate the Soviet Union and set the stage for American power in the post-war era."

"It's a complicated issue that has been simplified to the point of distortion," said Sherwin in the *Sun* interview, adding in reference to U.S. veterans' complaints about the Smithsonian display, "I think what we have is a rising tide of neo-McCarthyism that is reflected in this issue."

At his secluded home in southeast Aldergrove, Bill Franklin shakes his head in stunned disbelief at this quote. After a few moments of gathering his composure, he quietly compares it to Nazi holocaust deniers: "Those people are all the same, single-minded; they don't listen to anyone else but themselves…they weren't there."

The 75 year old Franklin, former RAF corporal and Japanese prisoner of war, speaks from real experience as a survivor of the "Fat Boy" A-bomb that fell on Nagasaki 50 years ago. Relatively fit of body and supremely sound of mind (during a three hour interview with *The Star* he effortlessly performs a math calculation in his head that would have most of us reaching for a pocket calculator), Franklin said he's grateful that the west's relations with Japan are now excellent, but he'll never forgive nor forget what Imperial Japan did to him and countless others before that 1945 surrender. He's still angry that he's never received an apology for his treatment at the hands of the Japanese army, let alone a financial reparation, and the efforts of revisionists like Sherwin only throw salt on an old wound.

Born September 29, 1919, in Oxford, England, Franklin recalls physicist Dr. Tom Marsland took a room in his parents' home next to the university campus, where Franklin's father, Edwin worked as a gardener. "Scientists at Oxford were the first to split the atom," said Franklin. "One day in the fall of 1929, Mr. Marsland came home and told us that it would have uses in medicine, industry…or destruction. It was ironic that I would wait all those years to witness it used in destruction."

Franklin joined the Royal Air Force reserve on June 1, 1939, fully expecting to be dispatched to the hostilities which were simmering in Europe over the growing imperialism of Adolf Hitler. "The British needed to build a force right away, and I was allocated to the trade of a storekeeper with a supply unit. We were mobilized three days before World War II was declared against Germany, and I was sent to #2 Flying Training School at Brize Norton," which later became a main U.S. bomber base. The underground hangars sheltered many prototypes which were tested and developed, such as the Sterlings, Halifax (later called Lancaster) bombers, "and a jet which never made service during the war." He also saw development of the blockbuster and dambuster bombs, before receiving new orders in October 1941 to "join the 242 Squadron and assemble stores for shipment overseas, destination unknown."

On their departure, December 8, the three squadrons (#242, 258, 604) in Fighter Wing #266, along with 20,000 fully mechanized troops formed a huge convoy of 90 ships destined for Malta or North Africa. "Fifty Hurricanes were allocated to us but we never saw, never met the pilots again. The Hurricanes were held in Malta; seven were shot down the first day (long before Franklin's ship convoy was due to arrive).

"It was touch and go all the way through. We were just one step ahead to win the war," said Franklin. "It was a terrible affair."

Half an hour before the ship convoy was due to enter Gibraltar, they got new orders to swing to the south. "We spent Christmas in Africa, in Sierra Leone, with a burnt-out main bearing due to a bad gale. We'd survived five days of 90 foot waves," said Franklin. "Very few of the men made mess halls, except for me, I never missed a meal."

Then in Capetown, South Africa, the men got five days shore leave before heading out again. With Rommel's Afrika Korps taking a heavy toll on the Allies, Franklin thought they were headed for Egypt, but the course was set for the Dutch East Indies. "We had stores aboard to be self-sufficient for two years."

The Japanese had surprise attacked Americans at Hawaii's Pearl Harbour, December 7, 1941, the day before Franklin's convoy left Scotland, which brought Japan, Asia and the U.S. into the war. In less than two months, Japan had invaded Malay, Philippines, Borneo, Hong Kong and Burma, followed by Singapore's collapse on February 15. "Half our troops were sent to Singapore, putting into Java, while the main squad continued to Sumatra. We put up a defence of Singapore with long-range tanks on the Hurricanes, but after the Japanese attacked Palembang, Sumatra, our boys withdrew back to Java."

Long before the war, the Japanese had taken advantage of complacency to establish numerous land and island bases throughout the region, which was a critical means by which they exacted a heavy toll on the Allies sent there. "We just didn't get the equipment," said Franklin. "A rifle was no good." All of Singapore's heavy guns were aimed to the sea, and useless against the Japanese forces who took the city overland. "For 17 days we did a terrific job, which enabled the second Allied convoy to reinforce northern Australia."

The British had lost battleships *Repulse* and *Prince of Wales*, and *HMS Exeter*, forced to sail without ammunition, was scuttled by the crew who didn't want the Japanese to get their hands on its radar equipment—one thing the Japanese did not yet have, even though the Japanese navy had been mainly built with British help before the war. "The Japanese were furious and left our boys in the sea for 72 hours before bringing them aboard. Several men who were hanging onto the lifeboats were lost to the sharks." Franklin was among the men who marched to Java's south coast for a planned rendezvous with the *Exeter*, not knowing it sat on the bottom of the ocean.

There were heavy losses on both sides in the furious campaign in the Java Sea, but by March 8, 1942, the Dutch East Indies capitulated, and the Japanese claimed as prisoners 98,000 Allied troops (including 5,000 U.S., British and Australian). From March to September, Franklin and the other prisoners repaired aerodromes in Java, then were moved to Batavia where they cleared jungle and planted tapioca with their bare hands. While none of the prisoners revealed their rank or trade, Franklin said, " the Japanese did a 'pretty' good job of determining our skills…I think they must have got hold of a gazette from a British library." Technical men were shipped to Singapore in September, and after six weeks in the jungle, Franklin was among the men shipped on the *Kama Kura Maru* to Nagasaki, where he arrived December 8, 1942, exactly one year after departure from Scotland.

There were about 1,500 men in the barracks, including 108 from the *Exeter*, some Dutch naval ratings and army, Javanese and Americans from the 8th Army and submarines. "We were slave labour in the docks, working on transport ships—no work, no Red Cross parcels. There was a parcel shipped every month for every man, but in the two years and eight months I was there we received only three and a half parcels each; whatever the Japanese army left after they picked through them.

"Our diet was 800 grams of rice and seaweed a day, plus vegetables in season, mainly digon, a sort of parsnip-turnip. Nothing with protein till the rice was short and they supplemented it with soybeans. Two times we got salmon, but riddled with bug holes through it, and two times tuna and whalemeat."

Beatings were commonplace, and reasons for them were never given. Franklin's buttocks were beaten black and blue by a guard with a pickaxe handle, and he was hit in the chest with the stock of a rifle. Workplace injuries were also common for the prisoners and the Japanese civilian workers brought into the docks, although Franklin is now receiving a British pension for a leg injury he suffered there, which recently developed into osteomyelitis. Seventy percent of the men in his POW barracks died from the abusive treatment before they were liberated, although many took out revenge in the form of sabotage in the docks.

"We were building new ships, south of the naval docks, opposite to the quayside. We worked every day, ten hours, except one day a month when we cleaned up camp. Each of us got a small coin for the labour every day, but the Korean men who carried loads of rocks from the cliffs to reclaim land out in the bay worked in pairs and they had to share a coin between the two of them. The Korean women had it worst; I felt very badly for them. There were 60,000 Korean women who had to clean out the brigs by day, a horrible job in itself, and then be "comfort women"—sex slaves for the Japanese army at night," said Franklin.

The morning of the A-bomb was like any other, except that Franklin noticed reconnaissance planes flying over while they were walking to the docks. "At 7 a.m. we were put to work, and we estimated it was about ten to 11 a.m. when it exploded about 100 metres above the city. It was about five miles away and I was inside a dry-dock capable of holding the Queen Mary, 60 feet below ground level. A light, an absolutely blinding white light—at first I thought a transformer had blown, but I couldn't hear any noise. The blast then blew out the superstructure; it was all floating above me. It was a thousand feet to the steps out and I feared the gate would give way and let the ocean into the dry-dock. But the pressure across the top of the dock formed a vacuum and I couldn't move, I was suspended there, then came the heat, terrific, overpowering, I thought I was going to be scorched to death. Then the pressure released and I nearly fell on my face. I was dodging falling debris, climbed out and reached the road, and saw the column of smoke rising and ran back to camp two miles away. The rear walls of the barracks had been blown in by the ricochet off the cliffs," said Franklin.

"The men were alongside the shelters of the camp watching this "mushroom" column building—I don't think we lost one POW in the blast. I'm still amazed by that. It took five days before the wind really removed the mushroom cloud."

"It was quite a hot summer, but cloudy that day, which is probably why Nagasaki was chosen. Even a match could have destroyed it, I still say, because it was dry as tinder and everything was built of wood and paper."

"We were ordered to the docks next day and given shovels to make slit trenches in case of further attack, but within half an hour were called back to camp. Enroute we encountered many injured on stretchers; they had areas of flesh like charcoal, falling off the bones like fillets. I was lucky to have been in St. John's before the war and had my nursing certificate, but some of the other men were sick at the sight."

"One morning the guards vanished, and the Dutch took over August 15 and posted guards. On August 31, the U.S. dropped supplies; each drop was three huge steel barrels welded together, filled with chocolate, toothpaste and soap. The impact was so great they split open, mixing everything together. Little children scooped out handfuls, eating it all up—I really felt sorry for them. I was down to 84 pounds at that time, lost 48 percent of my normal body weight. Everyone was so hungry that we over-fed, put on weight much too fast."

"The U.S. sailed in September 11 and the admiral of the Fleet went to our camp that evening. Three severe cases of TB were taken immediately to fly home and on September 13 we went to the quayside. Within 48 hours they had built a decontamination centre with a hospital ship alongside and we were put through hot water scrubbings. We were given clean clothes and a Bible and five days later we were put on the *U.S.S. Chenanago* for Okinawa. Just three days out we narrowly missed a mine, which was then detonated by a destroyer. We failed land because of an oncoming typhoon with 180 mile per hour winds that we sailed through for five days. When we returned to Okinawa the tent city was flattened."

"We were flown to the Philippines in a Liberator—Clark Field had literally hundreds of bombers and fighters lined up for an attack on Japan. We transferred to a Dakota to Manila, beat a rainstorm to land, and spent two weeks on *HMS Implacable*, a carrier-hospital boat to Vancouver. There we got treatments for our weight—one week of solid protein, all meat was hard to take, but it did help."

Franklin was put on the CN train to Halifax, then the *Isle de France* to Southampton, attended a memorable banquet in the Midlands, and endured further medical checks before discharge in February 1946. He returned to his job at Alden Press, where he fondly remembers binding T.E. Lawrence's *Seven Pillars of Wisdom*, before opening a green grocer with his brother. He emigrated to Canada, coming to Victoria in September 1948, and from 1953 to retirement in 1984, he rose to a superintendent's position with B.C. Forest Products. This job took him across the continent and around the world, but he settled in Aldergrove in 1973.

His first marriage dissolved in the '60s: "We were strangers after the war was over. POWs were only allowed to send facsimile postcards, with messages like, "We are being treated well" and only three of these got through in all that time anyway." They remained friendly after the divorce and she worked at the University of Victoria and stayed in contact with Franklin and their children until Lou Gehrig's disease claimed her. Franklin's second wife was taken away shortly after their marriage by cancerous tumours, and he then took Phyllis as his third wife after she lost her first husband to cancer at about the same time.

Bill and Phyllis have been together about 17 years now, involved in such organizations as Aldergrove Agricultural Association and Alder Grove Heritage Society. While *The Star* was interviewing Franklin, July 27, Phyllis was visiting AGHS secretary  Dora Chapman, seriously ill with cancer in MSA Hospital. *The Star* asked him if he didn't find it ironic that the A-bomb didn't cause him to die of cancers, while others who weren't there are suffering from cancers.

Franklin said that a couple of years ago he was diagnosed with prostate and bladder cancer, although the prostate cancer was dormant and left alone. He's received treatments for the bladder cancer, including two radioactive washes, and has since been diagnosed as free and clear of cancer. Franklin says he strongly believes in the peaceful uses of nuclear power, and foresees a future world that will be more environmentally friendly with it being used to incinerate sewage and other pollutants.

He never wants to see it used again in warfare but doesn't feel that the Americans have anything to apologize for either. Just as brutality is brutal, war is war, and as the samurai believe, all is fair in war. It was simply a roll of the dice that decided who lived and died, and Franklin happened to be one of the lucky ones who survived it. However, he gets angry at the historical revisionists who fault the Americans, and also feels they are poisoning the minds of those who have still not accepted part of the blame for the war and its atrocities. The Korean "comfort women" have only just this year received a grudging apology from the Japanese government, and a financial reparation program for the women has been launched by private Japanese citizens without government contribution. The Japanese Labourers Survivors Association of Great Britain, of which Franklin is a member, has yet to receive a settlement from Japan's government, and the same goes for claims from the Australians, New Zealanders, Dutch and Americans. "Our (Canada's) government doesn't stand behind us, but Britain does," said Franklin, "There's still 13,500 survivors and widows involved in the claim."

In March 1945, Americans firebombed Japanese cities with a form of napalm, which in Tokyo alone killed more than 100,000 people in one day, but still there was no surrender forthcoming. "Was being burned or boiled alive in Tokyo any better than being incinerated in Nagasaki? The Japanese were secretly experimenting with germ warfare in Manchuria. The Germans split the atom in 1937; can you imagine if the Germans or Britain got the bomb first? And the Allies expected to lose up to a million men in the invasion of Japan; thankfully, we didn't have to do that."

As far as Franklin is concerned the Nagasaki bomb finally and decisively ended the war, probably saved his life, and if it deterred others such as the Soviets from using it on civilian targets over the past 50 years, that's a real bonus. Historical revisionists may have 20-20 vision, but it's all hindsight.

Frank said he called organizers of a peace vigil planned for August 6 at Abbotsford City Hall, which is to commemorate the bombing with a survivor of Nagasaki as a speaker. Franklin was offended that he was given the brush-off by someone indifferent to his point of view, but he says he's not interested in confrontation and will stay away if he's not welcome. Instead he's going to the Aldergrove Legion's V-J Day ceremony, a parade and service followed by lunch on Sunday, August 13.

Franklin is looking forward to a lengthy retirement, filling his time with woodworking projects that are the envy of master craftsmen. He really doesn't want to dredge up old grievances, but says the current "politically correct" debate about Hiroshima and Nagasaki needs some balance from someone who was there.

ISBN 141206004-4